"Fernando Arzola Jr.'s book, *Toward a Prophetic Youth Ministry: Theory and Praxis in Urban Context*, is brilliantly and broadly conceived. Holistic, in the best sense of the word, informed by theology, theory and praxis, this book lays a solid foundation for effective urban ministry of any kind, but especially youth ministry. I recommend it to those considering working in urban youth ministry, as well as those currently working in this field."

JOHN M. PERKINS, PRESIDENT, THE JOHN M. PERKINS FOUNDATION

"A comprehensive study full of insight for urban youth ministry drawn from many disciplines. Important, challenging, holistic and solidly biblical. Highly recommended!"

DR. RONALD J. SIDER, PRESIDENT, EVANGELICALS FOR SOCIAL ACTION, PROFESSOR OF THEOLOGY, HOLISTIC MINISTRY AND PUBLIC POLICY, PALMER THEOLOGICAL SEMINARY, EASTERN UNIVERSITY

"Rather than trashing folks who see and do ministry differently than he does, Fernando Arzola Jr. has discovered the strengths of a wide variety of urban youth ministries and integrated them in a way that will both affirm and challenge all of us who love city kids in the name of Jesus. Here is a book born not only of practical experience and research, but also of deep and careful reflection, which takes seriously both personal discipleship and social justice in the inner city. Pay attention to Fernando Arzola."

BART CAMPOLO, FOUNDER, MISSION YEAR, FOUNDER, THE LAUNDROMAT PROJECT

"An urgent and creative contribution to the all-important field of youth ministry."

REVEREND DR. VIRGILO ELIZONDO, FOUNDING MEMBER, MEXICAN AMERICAN CULTURAL CENTER, TIME *MAGAZINE'S TOP 100 INNOVATORS, VISIONARIES FOR THE NEW MILLENNIUM*

"At last, an ethnic evangelical voice from the city stands on his urban academic platform and calls youth ministry to rethink its mission in the city and beyond. Fernando Arzola Jr.'s *Toward a Prophetic Youth Ministry: Theory and Praxis in Urban Context* stands in line with the many urban precedences that have shaped youth ministry as we know it today."

DR. MARK H. SENTER III, CHAIR, EDUCATIONAL MINISTRIES DEPARTMENT, TRINITY EVANGELICAL DIVINITY SCHOOL

"Fernando Arzola Jr.'s book is brilliant, insightful and well-written. In the often mysterious world of urban youth culture, Arzola stands out as a thoughtful leader and as a truly prophetic voice. This book is a necessary read for all who practice youth ministry in metro areas across the nation."

CHRISTOPHER B. BROOKS, NATIONAL COORDINATOR, URBNET

"Fernando Arzola Jr.'s *Toward a Prophetic Youth Ministry* is a fresh and provocative new voice in youth ministry—a much-needed *urban* voice in the critical youth ministry dialogue. Arzola's book promises to be a significant contribution to the literature of youth ministry; but more importantly, if its prophetic words are heeded it will bring about a holistic transformation of our youth."

DR. ELDIN VILLAFAÑE, PROFESSOR OF CHRISTIAN SOCIAL ETHICS, GORDON-CONWELL THEOLOGICAL SEMINARY

"Fernando Arzola Jr.'s seminal work is essential reading for all those committed to transformative and prophetic youth ministry both within and outside of cities globally. This is a well-researched volume with wide-ranging theoretical and practical implications for those called to equip youth as prophets for the Christian church and wider society."

DR. ROBERT W. PAZMIÑO, VALERIA STONE PROFESSOR OF CHRISTIAN EDUCATION, ANDOVER NEWTON THEOLOGICAL SCHOOL, TRINITY EVANGELICAL DIVINITY SCHOOL

"Finally! Something new to the field of youth ministry. A must read for anyone that wants to deal with young people in a comprehensive and holistic manner."

REVEREND DR. RAYMOND RIVERA, FOUNDER AND PRESIDENT, LATINO PASTORAL ACTION CENTER, BRONX, NEW YORK

"Arzola's is a strong voice from within the urban community, providing what only an insider can. He gives an honest tour of the strengths and weaknesses of urban life and its intersection with youth ministry. Arzola offers a resource that flips the script, contributing insight and an urban voice that may also be reinterpreted for suburban contexts. Finally, an urban youth ministry book that is suited for both academic courses and lay readers. It offers an excellent use of research, theory and substance from real-life insight."

AMY ELIZABETH JACOBER, PH.D., ASSOCIATE PROFESSOR OF PRACTICAL THEOLOGY/ YOUTH MINISTRY, TRUETT THEOLOGICAL SEMINARY

"Finally someone is writing with a specific and critical eye toward what it means to do holistic youth ministry in urban contexts. Professor Arzola offers a keen and necessary analysis of various paradigms of urban youth ministry. This work is important for at least two reasons: One, it fills a void. Not many scholars have written with both the city and its youth in focus. Two, it offers a view toward youth ministry that seeks to transform both persons and places. The call of God's prophets was to bring justice through rebuilding lives, restoring cities, and caring for orphans, widows, aliens, and the displaced. Arzola challenges us to think about what it means to do "prophetic youth ministry" in the inner city. I highly recommend this book to all who care about being agents of justice in a world plagued with injustice."

CALENTHIA S. DOWDY, ASSOCIATE PROFESSOR OF YOUTH MINISTRY AND CULTURE, EASTERN UNIVERSITY

"An excellent analysis moving our attention away from the merely programmatic concerns of youth ministry to more foundational ones. Sound theology accompanies thoughtful illustration and evidence of thinking outside the box. What grabbed my attention was Arzola's model descriptions and his thoughtful illustration of what a Prophetic Youth Ministry is as a paradigm for engaging the rapid, multidimensional and multicultural growth in the urban context. It challenges youth ministers and those concerned with youth in general to discern what is vital and essential in their youth ministry leadership in order to contribute meaningfully and constructively to the new communities being formed. While it is a book that is connected to those in urban areas, Arzola clearly articulates a future that will demand greater moral imagination and prophetic will if we are to respect the dignity of every young person that God allows us to impact. I found it to be a pragmatic assessment that actually is quite hopeful. *A must-have book in every pastoral library.*"

REVEREND HIRAM RIOS, PASTOR, GRACE FELLOWSHIP CHURCH, FLORIDA, AND REVEREND DR. ELIZABETH D. RIOS, CO-PASTOR, GRACE FELLOWSHIP CHURCH, FLORIDA, FOUNDER, CENTER FOR EMERGING FEMALE LEADERSHIP, CONTRIBUTING EDITOR, *PRISM MAGAZINE*

"Finally! A comprehensive analysis of current urban youth ministry models, with a clear presentation of developing a balanced approach for reaching young people in the city."

DR. TOMMY CARRINGTON, PRESIDENT, URBAN TRAINING NETWORK, ADJUNCT PROFESSOR, TRINITY INTERNATIONAL UNIVERSITY/PALM BEACH ATLANTIC UNIVERSITY

"A timely, truly interdisciplinary study, which tackles one of the most pressing issues of our times. When urban centers attract the largest segments of our population, and when our youth—urban or otherwise—count less with their parents' presence (taken away by an insatiably time-swallowing labor market, in order to make ends meet) or with public resources (sucked away by a frenzy of lowering taxes and privatization), the life-saving role of the churches is back at the center of social life. Arzola's book provides a compass for our churches to face the challenges posed by such a novel predicament of our urban youth—and he does it with both the contributions of his predecessors in mind, as well as a diverse, multiethnic, changing youth and readership in the horizon."

DR. OTTO MADURO, PROFESSOR OF WORLD CHRISTIANITY, DREW UNIVERSITY THEOLOGICAL SCHOOL

Toward a Prophetic Youth Ministry

THEORY AND PRAXIS IN URBAN CONTEXT

Fernando Arzola Jr.

IVP Academic
An imprint of InterVarsity Press
Downers Grove, Illinois

InterVarsity Press
P.O. Box 1400, Downers Grove, IL 60515-1426
World Wide Web: www.ivpress.com
E-mail: email@ivpress.com

InterVarsity Press® is the book-publishing division of InterVarsity Christian Fellowship/USA®, a student movement active on campus at hundreds of universities, colleges and schools of nursing in the United States of America, and a member movement of the International Fellowship of Evangelical Students. For information about local and regional activities, write Public Relations Dept., InterVarsity Christian Fellowship/USA, 6400 Schroeder Rd., P.O. Box 7895, Madison, WI 53707-7895, or visit the IVCF website at <www.intervarsity.org>.

All Scripture quotations, unless otherwise indicated, are taken from the Holy Bible, New International Version®, NIV®. *Copyright ©1973, 1978, 1984 by International Bible Society. Used by permission of Zondervan Publishing House. All rights reserved.*

Design: Cindy Kiple
Images: Keith Goldstein/Getty Images

ISBN 978-0-8308-2802-9

Printed in the United States of America ∞

Library of Congress Cataloging-in-Publication Data

Arzola, Fernando.
  Toward a prophetic youth ministry: theory and praxis in urban
  context/Fernando Arzola
    p. cm.
  Includes bibliographical references and index.
  ISBN 978-0-8308-2802-9
  1. Church work with youth—United States. 2. Urban youth—Religious
life—United States. I. Title.
  BV4447.A79 2008
  259'.230973091732—dc22

                                   2007043217

| P | 21 | 20 | 19 | 18 | 17 | 16 | 15 | 14 | 13 | 12 | 11 | 10 | 9 | 8 | 7 | 6 | 5 | 4 | 3 | 2 | 1 |
| Y | 26 | 25 | 24 | 23 | 22 | 21 | 20 | 19 | 18 | 17 | 16 | 15 | 14 | 13 | 12 | 11 | 10 | 09 | 08 | | | |

Contents

Preface

Often-heard frustrations for urban youth workers are the lack of appropriate resources and absence of models that are relevant for the urban context. It seems that urban ministers are frequently adapting material. Naturally, the majority of youth ministry resources are geared toward general adolescent spirituality. Ironically, this also adds to the frustration. The resources tend to present generalized spiritual insight without taking into account the sociological and anthropological distinctives of the culture of urban youth.

Furthermore, as of this writing, there is sparse literature which deals with urban youth ministry from an academic perspective. While there is a growing interest in hip-hop culture and the hip-hop church, this text does not address that particular topic.[1] Likewise, there is a body of writing addressing urban ministry in general, but very little commentary specifically on urban youth ministry.

AIM AND HOPE

The aim of *Toward a Prophetic Youth Ministry* is to provide a theoretical and methodological framework for understanding youth ministry in the urban context. My hope is fourfold: (1) that this work may make a helpful

---

[1]For further reflection on hip-hop culture and the church, see Alex Gee and John. E. Teeter, *Jesus and the Hip-Hop Prophets: Spiritual Insights from Lauryn Hill and Tupac Shakur* (Downers Grove, Ill.: InterVarsity Press, 2003); Calenthia S. Dowdy, "Voices from the Fringes: A Case for Prophetic Youth Ministry," *The Journal of Youth Ministry* 3, no. 2 (2005): 85-96; Timothy Holder, *The Hip Hop Prayer Book* (New York: Church Publishing, 2006); Efrem Smith and Phil Jackson, *The Hip-Hop Church: Connecting with the Movement Shaping Our Culture* (Downers Grove, Ill.: InterVarsity Press, 2006).

contribution to the field of youth ministry education by deepening the scholarly reflection and dialogue of urban youth ministry; (2) that prophetic youth workers in the urban context feel affirmed, empowered and energized to continue this most holy and important work; (3) that traditional, liberal and activist youth workers consider moving toward nurturing more prophetic youth ministry paradigms; and (4) that urban youth ministries transform into dynamic and holistic youth ministries addressing the spiritual, personal and social needs of urban youth.

The book begins with a discussion of four paradigms of youth ministry presently operating in the urban context—traditional, liberal, activist and prophetic. In the second chapter I present five assumptions that undergird a prophetic youth ministry, with some comparison made to suburban and rural models. Then in chapter three I examine a six-part model for developing a more holistic and diversified urban youth ministry, based on the text of Luke 10:27. In chapter four I set forth a five-movement teaching method for biblical and cultural exegesis. The fifth chapter explores the philosophical and theological shifts that move an urban ministry in a prophetic direction.

Youth ministry, particularly in an urban context, is necessarily an interdisciplinary project, so the second section of the book explores various disciplines and their role in prophetic youth ministry. Chapter six introduces the idea of developing a multidisciplinary and praxis-oriented approach to youth ministry. Chapter seven focuses on adolescent developmental psychology, which chapter eight builds on in a presentation of recent research into the adolescent brain, as well as issues related to hormonal and physical development. Also important are the social sciences; chapter nine examines cultural and contextual realities of urban youth and how these inform urban youth ministry, while chapter ten considers various educational ideologies and in particular a radical educative perspective. The final chapter has the youth worker in view, offering an illustration of the role of the urban youth worker in a prophetic ministry in an urban context.

CLARIFYING SUBJECTIVITY AND LIMITATIONS

I confess this book is intentionally subjective. I believe the prophetic youth ministry paradigm is the most appropriate and effective type of youth ministry for the urban context. Therefore, I wish to share the following perspectives from which I stand in order for the reader to better understand my thinking.

- I use the term *prophetic* to express a spiritually and socially engaged ethic.
- I write from an inner-city urban context and for an inner-city urban context.
- As of this writing, my worldview is informed as a Puerto-Rican American raised in the Mott Haven section of the South Bronx and as a lifelong New York City resident.
- Recognizing the diversity of the urban context, my experiences and insight on urban youth ministry come primarily from Hispanic and black churches.
- While I have painfully attempted to keep this book as "close to the streets" as possible, it is written primarily in an academic and theoretical manner.
- I write from a biblically and historically orthodox tradition rooted in Holy Scripture and in the ancient creeds of the church.
- I address this subject more as a Christian religious educator than as a systematic theologian or someone seeking to do constructive theological work alongside contextual issues.

Acknowledgments

This book is based on lectures given at the 2004 Urban Youth Ministry Seminar sponsored by Nyack College at its Rockland campus. I am indebted to Dr. Ronald Belsterling for his invitation, without which these thoughts may never have been written.

I am grateful for the ongoing support and mentoring of Dr. Leonard Kageler. He is a wise counselor, a humble servant, a self-effacing leader and a role model for youth ministry educators.

I am eternally thankful for the Reverend Raymond Rivera, who served as my pastor and spiritual mentor when I rededicated my life to the Lord. It was also under Rivera's tutelage that I intentionally learned and incarnationally experienced holistic ministry and prophetic engagement.

I wish to acknowledge Dr. Luis Carlo, who opened the door for me to enter Nyack College and encouraged me in the early days of my academic career. He continues to be a strong bridge between the academy, the church and the community.

I am grateful to Dr. David Turk, who invested in my personal and academic leadership formation. Throughout my years at Nyack College he generously nurtured my professional development.

Professor Denise Hirschlein, friend, colleague and sister in Christ, was and remains a great supporter of my work. In particular, her encouragement during my doctoral work and the writing of this book was especially uplifting.

Of course, much of this book would not have been given form if it were not for the students at Nyack College and Alliance Theological Seminary who enrolled in my courses. Their expressed solidarity with the work and constructive feedback of its contents greatly informed my thinking.

Special thanks go to April Boland, proofreader extraordinaire. April provided objective editorial insight and thoughtful philosophical critique during the early drafts of the manuscript.

Acknowledgment with distinction goes to David A. Zimmerman, associate editor, InterVarsity Press. From beginning to end, Dave was a phenomenal guide and encourager to me during the publishing process. His suggestions on the manuscript were excellent—objective, challenging and insightful.

I am grateful for the work and affirmation of the Association of Youth Ministry Educators (AYME), an incredibly fun, faithful and scholarly group of youth workers turned professors. I am proud to be counted as one of them. Appreciation also goes to the North American Professors of Christian Education (NAPCE) for their steadfast commitment to nurturing Christian disciples.

I am humbled by the written words of those who provided public endorsement of this book. To all of you, thanks!

I would be remiss if I didn't send a "shout out" to The Coalition of Urban Youth Workers. The coalition is an association of evangelical youth workers from Greater New York that collaborate in city-wide and regional youth-engagement and leadership-development efforts.

Most important, I wish to thank my wife, Jill, for her love and continuous support of my work, and my daughter, Nicole, who has taught me more about youth ministry and adolescence than any teacher or resource ever has.

PART ONE

Prophetic Models and Perspectives

1

Urban Youth Ministry Archetypes

Contrary to popular belief, urban youth do not constitute a monolithic group. There is no one urban youth voice. Furthermore, there is no one model of urban youth ministry. Urban youth ministries have in common only three identifying components: (1) they are Christian, (2) they are located in the city, and (3) they minister to youth. Beyond this, urban youth ministries are as varied as the churches in the body of Christ. Nonetheless, because of these three common components, urban youth ministries reflect a unique stream within the dynamic and ever-changing river of youth ministries. Let us briefly examine three urban youth worker archetypes and the ministries in which they are engaged.

Anthony is the youth pastor of a theologically conservative church. He is primarily committed to the spiritual formation of youth. He prepares weekly Bible studies and youth outreach events, and has infused a dynamic spirit into worship. Anthony sees himself as pastor to the youth. He understands that the teens in his youth ministry come from poor families with social needs. He also recognizes the importance of personal and academic growth among youth. These matters, however, are secondary to their spiritual formation. For Anthony, the primary goal of the youth ministry is to bring youth into the Christian faith and to help them grow in their relationship with Jesus Christ.

Michelle is the director of youth ministry at a theologically liberal church. She is primarily committed to the personal development of youth. She prepares weekly lesson plans which address adolescent issues, promote diversity and provide for rap sessions allowing the group to discuss teen-related concerns. Michelle sees herself as a friend to the youth. She uses the Bible when preparing her lesson plans, but primarily as a reference. While she does teach about the Christian faith, Michelle believes that it is most important to help teens develop a healthy spirituality and respect for all religious traditions. She is concerned about the needs of people in the city and encourages the teens to become involved in charity work. Yet, for Michelle, the primary goal of the youth ministry is to help youth develop healthy self-esteem while becoming aware of their civic responsibilities.

John is the minister of youth at a church whose theology promotes a social gospel. He is primarily committed to social change. He prepares lessons which focus on empowerment issues, economic concerns and social engagement. John sees himself as an advocate for the youth. He certainly believes education is important and recognizes the significance of youth developing healthy self-esteem. The spiritual growth of youth is also important. However, for John, the primary goal of youth ministry is to empower and equip youth to recognize and respond to social and systemic injustices which confront teens as well as to encourage them to promote social change.

While these three types of workers reflect important streams within urban youth ministry, the overemphasis on any one tends to nurture a limited and unbalanced adolescent spirituality. Furthermore, each youth ministry tends to give birth to or nurture a particular type of teenager. In line with the ministries described above, I have encountered three general urban Christian youth archetypes. First is the dogmatic Christian youth archetype. These teenagers are loyal to denominational/spiritual traditions and understand Jesus as Lord and Savior. They read the Scriptures through a tradition-specific interpretive lens (Evangelical, Pentecostal, Charismatic, Baptist, Catholic, etc). Second is the intellectual Christian

Questions to Ponder

Reflect on the youth ministry in which you've been involved. What archetype did it tend to birth or nurture: dogmatic, intellectual or socially engaged Christian youth?

youth archetype. These teenagers are not necessarily more intelligent than the others; they are simply more oriented toward rational process. These teenagers understand Jesus as a good person and a wise sage. They read the Scriptures metaphorically. Finally is the socially engaged Christian youth archetype. The teenagers tend to be strongly ethnocentric, understanding Jesus as a radical social activist fighting for all cultural groups. They read the Scriptures from a social-justice perspective.

FOUR PARADIGMS OF YOUTH MINISTRY IN THE URBAN CONTEXT

The following is an attempt to present a typological analysis of four urban youth ministry paradigms. It is my hope that this may contribute to increased critical reflection and dialogue regarding youth ministry in the urban context.

In *Social Analysis: Linking Faith and Justice,* Joe Holland and Peter Henriot present a three-part model for better understanding social justice theory: (1) the traditional perspective, (2) the liberal perspective and (3) the radical perspective.[2] Each perspective, they argue, serves as a lens through which social justice is viewed. Because ministry in the urban context is so entwined with social engagement, I have adapted Holland and Henriot's helpful model to create a typology of urban youth ministries.[3]

In my own work I have observed four paradigms of youth ministry in the urban context: (1) the traditional youth ministry paradigm, (2) the liberal youth ministry paradigm, (3) the activist youth ministry paradigm and (4) the prophetic youth ministry paradigm. These paradigms reflect a way of understanding and ministering to youth in the urban setting. Each reflects a specific ministerial worldview with its own philosophical and theological assumptions.

Like all typologies, this one creates ideal classifications that can become overgeneralized and even problematic at times. Some traits may even overlap among the paradigms. Yet typological classifications can also help us

---

[2] Joe Holland and Peter Henriot, *Social Analysis: Linking Faith and Justice* (Maryknoll, N.Y.: Orbis/ Center of Concern, 1983).

[3] I am also indebted to Dr. Kieran Scott, professor at the Fordham University Graduate School of Religion and Religious Education, for his spring 2005 teachings regarding guiding principles and metaphors and their place in education and ministry.

Questions to Ponder

These paradigms reflect a way of understanding and ministering to youth in the urban setting. As you examine each one, ask yourself, Which most closely reflects my worldview of youth ministry in the city? What are the fundamental underpinnings of my perspective? What areas does my youth ministry need to strengthen? What areas does my youth ministry need to change? What assumptions do I have about youth ministry in the city? Am I asking the right questions? What is my primary concern for youth? What is my primary youth ministry image or metaphor? How do I deal with conflict? What aspect of my worldview do I need to transform?

see and better understand the fundamental differences among paradigms. Furthermore, the four paradigms may be applicable in other settings, particularly in some rural settings, where economic and social justice needs are especially acute.

Understanding these paradigms is useful to both youth ministry educators and urban youth workers. These paradigms offer youth ministry educators insights about four different approaches within the spectrum of urban youth ministries. They will also give educators a better understanding of the breadth of urban youth ministry thought. Urban youth workers may find these paradigms helpful in reexamining their own philosophical and theological underpinnings, engaging in ministerial reevaluation, and developing more holistic youth ministry programming.

1. The traditional youth ministry paradigm. The traditional youth ministry paradigm is one of the most common in the urban context. The emphasis in this paradigm is on *youth ministry* in the urban context. That is, its primary purpose is developing a ministry-centered program for urban youth. Each model has a primary question when evaluating the ministry. Because of its emphasis on programs, the evaluative question for this paradigm is, How effective are the programs in the youth ministry? This question is ministerial in nature. It focuses on the programs *for* youth. The focus and assumptions of this model begin with *ministry programs,* then pursue how they may be addressed to youth. The traditional urban youth minister asks, What programs/curricula are best or most effective for our youth?

The primary concern for the traditional youth ministry is, first and foremost, the spiritual needs of urban youth. Therefore, traditional youth ministries will focus on spiritual formation through their particular tradition-specific perspective (Evangelical, Pentecostal, Charismatic, Baptist, Orthodox, Catholic, etc). Programmatically, this is manifested in Bible studies, worship/liturgical services, religious education, Sunday school—all the "spiritual" components of youth ministry. Traditional youth ministry retreats are developed, presumably, to help urban youth nurture their relationships with Christ.

The use of a guiding principle is essential to every philosophy of youth ministry. For the traditional youth ministry, the root principle is *discipleship*, to become disciples of Christ. Naturally, the issue here with the traditional paradigm is not the emphasis on discipleship, which should be present in any good Christian ministry paradigm, but the *exclusive* emphasis on discipleship as primarily an individual, personal change with little impact in the social realm.

The traditional youth ministry is based on an ideology of *biology*, a growing healthy body—youth ministry as the body of Christ. Therefore, the traditional paradigm believes the body of youth ministry, as an institution, and its traditions, should be preserved.

Holland and Henriot explore how conflict is addressed by the various perspectives. How does the traditional youth ministry respond to conflict?[4] Because of its commitment to tradition and order, the traditional youth ministry tends to avoid or silence conflict. At its worst, conflict is viewed as inappropriate, wrong and even deviant. Therefore, the traditional response to conflict tends to be "authoritarian."[5]

At its best, the traditional youth ministry challenges us to be rooted in the life and teachings of Jesus Christ. At its worst, it is more concerned with winning souls, indoctrination into a specific tradition and engaging in spiritual warfare at the expense of addressing the social injustices of this world.

Each paradigm is exemplified in the New Testament. While no one

---

[4]Holland and Henriot, *Social Analysis*, pp. 31-45.
[5]Ibid.

group can fully represent the paradigm, identification of a particular biblical group serves as a helpful reference in better understanding each of the typologies. The traditional youth ministry is most exemplified in the Pharisees. At first glance, this appears insulting, but a broader understanding of the Pharisees is in order. The Pharisees represented a political-religious Jewish group who believed in separating themselves from their non-Jewish neighbors. And, while they have gotten a bad rap over the centuries, the Pharisees were faithful Jews, committed to the teachings of the Torah and struggling to live a life of moral purity—not unlike biblically orthodox Christians today. However, the Pharisees, at least as they are characterized in the New Testament, had a tendency toward legalism, a literal interpretation of the Scriptures and a strict, almost fanatical observance of the teachings of the law.

2. The liberal youth ministry paradigm. The liberal youth ministry is very popular with mainline denominational churches, particularly within middle-class and upper-middle-class neighborhoods. This is also seen in inner-city neighborhoods with churches that are led by theologically liberal pastors. The emphasis of this paradigm is on *compassionate ministry* for urban youth. That is, its primary purpose is developing a felt-needs ministry-centered programming for urban youth. This paradigm begins with the *felt needs* of youth and then addresses them through youth ministry programs.

Because of the liberal youth ministry's compassionate perspective, its evaluative question is, How are the needs of urban youth effectively being met? This question is psychological and developmental in nature. It focuses on the needs *of* youth.

The primary concern for the liberal youth ministry is the personal and emotional needs of urban youth. Therefore, programmatically, the liberal youth ministry will tend to offer interrelational and intrarelational therapeutic programs. These programs include support groups, mentoring, family-based initiatives, intergenerational activities, trips, arts and crafts, and choirs. Liberal youth ministry retreats are developed to help urban youth better understand themselves and their uniqueness and to nurture a healthier self-awareness.

The guiding principle for the liberal youth ministry is *growth*. Philosophically, the metaphor of growth is rooted in progressive education. Are urban youth growing in a healthy manner?

The liberal youth ministry is based on an ideology of *evolution*. That is, youth ministries need to change and adapt. Therefore, the liberal paradigm believes that youth ministry, as an institution, needs to be reformed.

How does the liberal youth ministry tend to respond to conflict? It understands conflict as part of the evolutionary process for ministry and relationships. Therefore, the liberal response to conflict tends to be *managerial*. This is particularly seen in the emphasis on conflict management or conflict resolution.

At its best, the liberal youth ministry paradigm challenges us to address the personal and emotional needs of youth. At its worst, it tends to overemphasize the humanity of Jesus at the expense of the divinity of Christ, who is Son of God. Also, middle-class urban youth ministries may not fully appreciate the suffering realities of their urban sisters and brothers in the inner city.

The liberal youth ministry is analogous to the Sadducees. The Sadducees did not believe in the resurrection of the dead, the immortality of the soul and the existence of angels. They were the sophisticates, highly educated and, generally speaking, the most intellectual. They were strongly opposed, on the one hand, by the Pharisees, for not being faithful to Jewish teachings and, on the other hand, by the Zealots, for being overly accommodating to Greek culture.

Like the Sadducees, the liberal youth ministry is committed to personal growth, intellectual development and emotional well-being. The liberal youth ministry tends to view Christianity more as a philosophy of life rather than as a personal relationship with Jesus Christ. Youth who participate in the liberal youth ministry may be taught the Scriptures respectfully, but largely metaphorically, with less emphasis on its divinely authoritative significance. Also, the Christian faith tends to be presented as principles for ethical living instead of biblical guidelines for living a holy and righteous life pleasing unto God.

3. The activist youth ministry paradigm. The activist youth ministry paradigm is the third type found in many inner-city urban churches. The emphasis of this paradigm is on *urban ministry* for youth. That is, its primary purpose is developing an urban-ministry-centered program for youth. The paradigm begins by identifying *urban issues* affecting youth then develops appropriate youth ministry programs which address these issues or needs.

Because of the activist youth ministry's contextual concerns, its evaluative question is, How are the issues which affect urban youth effectively being responded to? This question is sociological and anthropological in nature. It focuses on the needs experienced *by* youth.

The primary concern for the activist youth ministry is the social needs of urban youth. Therefore, in order to meet these many needs, the activist youth ministry tends to offer after-school programs, economic empowerment programs, job training and social justice initiatives. Activist youth ministry retreats are offered to help urban youth develop trust in each other and work better together as a group to more intentionally develop social interaction abilities and reduce at-risk behavior.

The guiding principle for the activist youth ministry is *justice.* What are the injustices suffered by urban youth? How can justice be actualized for urban youth?

The activist youth ministry is based on an ideology of *revolution.* Therefore, the activist paradigm believes that youth ministry, as an institution, should be deconstructed and reconstructed. For the activist, the traditional paradigm is out of touch and irrelevant and the liberal paradigm is weak and insufficient.

How does the activist youth ministry respond to conflict? It expects conflict in confronting social issues and even creates conflict if it may lead to social change. Therefore, the activist response to conflict tends to be *negotiational,* not unlike a union representative negotiating on behalf of his or her membership. It may also be *confrontational,* if this confrontation may lead to revolutionary change.

At its best, the activist youth ministry challenges us to be engaged in addressing systemic injustice and social sin. At its worst, it seems overly concerned with deconstructing traditions, fighting systems and overturning institutions rather than growing in Christ.

The activist youth ministry is best exemplified by the Zealots. The Zealots were a radical Jewish group that was engaged in, or at least supported, the overthrow of the Roman government that occupied the Jewish land. They also abhorred the influence of Greek culture within Jewish life. This group, perhaps more than any other Jewish sect, awaited a revolutionary messiah who would free the Jews from spiritual and social bondage.

The activist youth ministry surely promotes a revolutionary Jesus and nurtures—to a greater or lesser degree—revolutionary youth engaged in social change. The danger of an extremist brand of activist youth ministry is the development of a ministry rooted more in anger against structures and systems rather than in the compassion of Jesus Christ. Acts of justice may be manifested more in social revolution than in biblical transformation.

In theory, social change sounds good, but to what end? Not all social change is necessarily in keeping with the Bible's understanding of justice. Youth may become martyrs for the wrong cause. While involvement in social change is certainly an essential component of the Christian life, it must be centered on Christ and faithful to God's Word.

4. The prophetic youth ministry paradigm. Prophetic youth ministry is the most effective and holistic paradigm for ministering to urban youth. It is also the youth ministry paradigm least in operation in the urban context. The emphasis of this ministry is *Christian ministry* for urban youth. That is, its primary purpose is developing a *Christ-centered ministry* for urban youth. The assumptions of this paradigm begin with Christ then develop a ministry for youth.

This starting point is significant. The traditional youth ministry focuses on youth ministry programs. The liberal youth ministry focuses on the personal felt needs of youth. The activist youth ministry focuses on the social concerns affecting urban youth. While all these issues are important, the prophetic youth ministry does not begin with these. The heart of the prophetic youth ministry is Christ; from Christ the ministry reaches out to address all three of these needs.

Because of the prophetic youth ministry's Christ-centered perspective (instead of program-centered, felt-needs centered or urban-issues centered), its evaluative question is, How is Christ growing, deepening and manifesting *in* the lives of urban youth? This evaluative question shifts entirely the programmatic development of the youth ministry by focusing on

Table 1.1. Four Paradigms of Youth Ministry in the Urban Context

	Ministry emphasis	Purpose	Assumptions	Evaluative question	Primary concern	Programs	Guiding principle	Ideology	Change in youth ministry	Approach to conflict	Biblical example
Traditional youth ministry	**YOUTH MINISTRY** in the urban context	Ministry-centered programs for urban youth	Begins with youth ministry programs	How effective is the urban youth ministry program? This ministerial question focuses on the program *for* youth.	Spiritual needs of urban youth	Bible study, worship service, evangelism, fellowship, Sunday school	Discipleship	Biology	No change	Attempts to avoid and/or silence conflict	Pharisees
Liberal youth ministry	**MINISTRY** for urban youth	Felt-needs-centered programs for urban youth	Begins with felt needs of youth	How are the needs of urban youth effectively being met? This psychological question focuses on the needs *of* youth.	Personal needs of urban youth	Support groups, counseling, mentoring, choir, trips, family services, music and art	Growth	Evolution	Reform	Understands conflict as part of the evolutionary process	Sadducees

	Ministry emphasis	Purpose	Assumptions	Evaluative question	Primary concern	Programs	Guiding principle	Ideology	Change in youth ministry	Approach to conflict	Biblical example
Activist youth ministry	URBAN MINISTRY for youth	Urban-ministry-centered programs for youth	Begins with urban issues affecting youth	How are the issues which affect urban youth effectively being responded to? This sociological/anthropological question focuses on the issues experienced *by* youth.	Social needs of urban youth	Social action, after-school tutoring, ethnic celebrations, food pantry, economic empowerment, job training	Justice	Revolution	Deconstruct and reconstruct	Expects conflict by confronting social issues and even creates conflict if it may lead to change	Zealots
Prophetic youth ministry	CHRISTIAN MINISTRY for urban youth	Christ-centered programs for urban youth	Begins with Christ	How is Christ deepening, growing and manifesting in the lives of urban youth? The holistic question focuses on Christ *in* youth.	Spiritual needs of urban youth	Integrated spiritual, personal and social counseling programs	Transformation	Liberation	Transform	Believes conflict may be creative and even welcomes constructive dissonance	Prophets

Christ first and then considering programmatic questions second. The question allows for a more holistic and integrative approach—theoretically and programmatically. It focuses on Christ *in* youth.

Because of the holistic and integrative nature of the prophetic youth ministry, its concern for urban youth, too, is holistic and integrative. This paradigm seeks to address the spiritual, personal and social needs of urban youth. For the prophetic youth worker, to address only one of the three aspects over and above the others is nonsensical.

What critique does the prophetic youth worker offer regarding the traditional, liberal and activist youth ministries? (See table 1.1.) First, a traditional youth ministry may address the spiritual needs of urban youth, but does it help them deal with their personal and emotional needs? And, does it speak out on behalf of social justice? A youth ministry certainly needs to share the gospel message with teenagers and help them to grow in Christ (meeting spiritual needs). But, in many urban communities where schools are subpar, gang membership is growing, recreational sexual behavior is the norm and homes may be in disarray, youth ministries need to provide academic help, personal encouragement and emotional support (meeting personal needs). Youth ministries also need to intentionally interact and respond to the realities of poverty, discrimination, police brutality and other stressors (meeting social needs). Frankly, any youth ministry not engaged in helping to meet the personal and social needs of youth in their community will not be taken seriously by the neighborhood youth.

Many traditional youth ministries are now reaching out to youth in more nontraditional ways. They hold hip-hop concerts, minister in the neighborhood or sponsor sports tournaments. While these approaches are certainly very important and may be evangelistically effective, they do not make a youth ministry prophetic. For a traditional youth ministry to become more prophetic, it must also be engaged in the personal and social transformation of urban youth—whether or not they accept Christ. The prophetic paradigm affirms the traditional paradigm's commitment to the gospel message but challenges the traditional paradigm to become more engaged in meeting the personal and social needs of all urban youth.

Second, a liberal youth ministry may address the personal needs of urban youth, but does it help nurture a deepening and growing relationship with Jesus Christ? And, does it speak out on behalf of social injustice? Many liberal youth ministries, particularly liberal youth ministries in the inner city, tend to be engaged in meeting the personal and social needs of their youth. However, they also tend to soften the radical social message of Christ as well as the gospel message that the assurance of salvation comes through the life, death and resurrection of Jesus Christ. The prophetic paradigm affirms the liberal paradigm's commitment to the personal and charitable concerns of youth but challenges the liberal paradigm to be more faithful to the traditional and orthodox gospel message, as well as to become more radically engaged in social justice.

Finally, an activist youth ministry may address the social needs of urban youth, but does it help nurture a deepening and growing relationship with Jesus Christ? And, does it help deal with the many personal and emotional needs of youth? The prophetic paradigm certainly feels camaraderie with the activist paradigm's social commitment, but it challenges the activist paradigm to be more faithful to the traditional and orthodox understanding of the gospel. Certain activist youth ministries have championed causes outside the traditional understanding of biblical orthodoxy. Some activist youth leaders have even embraced behaviors, actions and worldviews that are in direct contradiction with an orthodox understanding of the Holy Bible. This is a departure from the message of the biblical prophets. On these matters, the prophets part ways with the zealots.

A prophetic youth ministry is committed to address all three components—spiritual, personal and social. Therefore, programmatically, it offers activities and initiatives that address all three components, integrating many of the programs listed in the three other paradigms. A job training initiative, GED preparation, tutoring service, group processing or mentoring programming is added to a Bible study, worship service or youth rally. Prophetic youth ministry retreats are developed to help youth better understand their relationship with themselves, with Christ and with others.

The guiding principle for the prophetic youth ministry is *transformation*. How can youth be transformed holistically—spiritually, personally and socially?

The word *trans* means to go beyond and on through to the other side. The word *form* comes from the Latin, *forma*, "beauty." *Transformation*, therefore, implies a reforming and reshaping of people toward the beautiful. A primary goal of the prophetic youth ministry is to remove the veil covering the soul of urban youth and show them how beautiful they really are. The call to transformation is to confront and transform the ugliness within ourselves (personal), within our hearts (spiritual) and within our society (social).

The prophetic youth ministry is based on an ideology of *liberation*. Therefore, youth ministries, as an institution, should be transformed. The traditional perspective believes no significant changes are necessary in youth ministries. The liberal perspective believes some changes are necessary in youth ministries. The activist perspective believes in a complete overhaul of youth ministries. The prophetic perspective believes in a paradigmatic transformation, a fundamental change of purpose, guiding principle, assumptions and evaluative questions. Liberation, unlike revolution, is not a rejection of the institution of youth ministry. Rather, liberation, as understood by this paradigm, is rooted in the trifold prophetic tension felt in honoring the apostolic tradition and casting an eschatological and existential vision, while standing in solidarity with urban youth, especially the poor and marginalized.

How does the prophetic youth ministry tend to respond to conflict? It believes conflict may be creative and even welcomes constructive dissonance. Therefore, the prophetic response to conflict tends to intentionally *name and engage conflict* toward transformation.

In "Voices from the Fringes: A Case for Prophetic Youth Ministry," Calenthia S. Dowdy affirms that the prophetic paradigm is needed. She writes,

> Current youth ministry must release and empower its young prophets, encouraging them to speak and act regarding both moral and social righteousness. . . . It would not be wise to discourage them from learning about and speaking about structural evil that systematically represses certain segments of society. . . . This is not a call to a "social gospel," rather it is a call to the *whole gospel*. All of Christ's message must be preached.[6]

---

[6]Calenthia S. Dowdy, "Voices from the Fringes: A Case for Prophetic Youth Ministry," *The Journal of Youth Ministry* 3, no. 2 (2005): 95.

The prophetic youth ministry paradigm is best exemplified by the prophets. The prophets were an unusual bunch. They were often misunderstood and disliked. They exhorted people to turn away from their sins and prepare for a day of judgment (spiritual repentance) and to change their way of living (personal repentance); the prophets challenged both spiritual and political leadership to initiate social justice (social repentance). Prophetic youth ministry is ministry on the margins, in the periphery. Prophetic youth workers are *peripheral prophets.* Dowdy distinguishes between what Robert Wilson identifies as *central prophets* and *peripheral prophets.* She writes,

> *Central prophets* are those who belong to the social center of the empire and customarily enjoy social prestige and political power. They tend to be concerned with the preservation of the status quo and are controlled by their governing constituencies. And then there are *peripheral prophets,* those who belong to the fringes of society. They lack social prestige and power and derive their authority either from God and/or some marginal group to which they may belong. These prophets fight for social change and quality of life issues for marginalized groups. They believe that all people, regardless of their station in life, deserve justice and wholeness. They speak bold proclamation to the ruling powers, denouncing structured violence and economic and social injustices.[7]

Like the prophets, the prophetic youth ministry envisions and develops a ministry which addresses the spiritual, personal and social needs of youth. A prophetic youth ministry endeavors to assist youth to grow in Christ, develop into ethical persons and become engaged in social action.

The prophetic youth ministry is built upon three interlocking philosophical and theological components: (1) a traditional understanding of the Holy Bible and Christian or-

Questions to Ponder

Reflect on the youth ministry in which you've been involved. Was it committed to understanding the Holy Bible and Christian orthodoxy? Was it committed to the spiritual, personal and emotional development of youth? Was it committed to social justice?

---

[7]Ibid., p. 89. See also Robert R. Wilson, *Prophecy and Society in Ancient Israel* (Minneapolis: Augsburg Fortress, 1980).

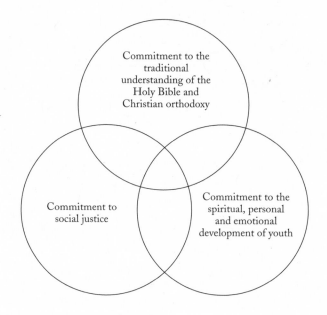

Figure 1.1. Three interlocking commitments of the prophetic youth ministry

thodoxy; (2) the spiritual, personal and emotional development of youth; and (3) social justice (see fig. 1.1).

DEFINING PROPHETIC YOUTH MINISTRY IN THE URBAN CONTEXT

A prophetic youth ministry is a Christ-centered ministry fundamentally committed to and intentionally engaged in the spiritual, personal and social liberation and transformation of urban youth and their communities.

A prophetic youth ministry is Christ-centered. A prophetic youth ministry is centered first and always on Christ. While all youth ministries claim to be Christ centered, the emphasis here is to distinguish the prophetic youth ministry from being programs centered, felt-needs centered or even youth centered. A program may not necessarily need to be Christ centered in order to be helpful or resourceful. However, if it is not Christ centered, then it is rooted in something else and, ultimately, can neither be holistically transformative nor be biblically prophetic.

A prophetic youth ministry is fundamentally holistic. A prophetic youth ministry is philosophically and constitutively committed to address the spiritual, personal and social needs of urban youth. A youth ministry which does not fundamentally root itself in all three of these components is not holistic.

A prophetic youth ministry is programmatically holistic. A prophetic youth ministry intentionally programs the youth ministry to meet the spiritual, personal and social needs of urban youth. A youth ministry which does not programmatically address all three of these components is not holistic.

A prophetic youth ministry engages its community. A prophetic youth ministry is committed to the transformation of its community, as well as the teens that enter the church. It does not isolate itself from the community. It is incarnationally involved in the spiritual, personal and social transformation of the community's youth.

A prophetic youth ministry is liberational. A prophetic youth ministry believes that Jesus Christ liberates urban youth, and all people, from personal and spiritual bondage, as well as social and systemic sin. It does not evangelize alone, without social action. And, it does not address social action alone, without evangelism.

A prophetic youth ministry promotes eschatological hope. A prophetic ministry recognizes that not all the promises will be fulfilled in this life but that it is demonstrating and pointing to the kingdom of God which will only be fully realized in the future. This eschatological hope is one thing that distinguishes the prophetic from both the liberal and the activist paradigms. A prophetic ministry succeeds when the prophetic message has been spoken and enacted, not just when it sees results in terms of actual liberation or change of social conditions. Yet this prophetic hope must be held without giving in to defeatism or inactivity.[8]

A prophetic youth ministry is transformational. A prophetic youth ministry believes transformation is a process toward the fulfillment of the reign of God, in and through the lives of urban youth. The prophetic youth ministry begins with liberation and proceeds with transformation, a lifelong spiritual, personal and social process.

---

[8]I am grateful to Dr. Thomas E. Bergler for his personal communication on this matter, July 14, 2006.

Third, develop a ministry
which intentionally meets
spiritual, personal and social needs of youth.

First, agree on the three
interlocking commit-
ments of the prophetic
youth ministry.

Transformation

Second, identify
the spiritual, personal
and social needs
of youth
in your target
community.

Figure 1.2. Steps in transformation toward a prophetic youth ministry

TOWARD A PROPHETIC YOUTH MINISTRY

How does a youth ministry move toward becoming a prophetic youth ministry? Fundamentally, there needs to be a paradigmatic shift both in worldview and in structure. There is no simple way of transitioning into a prophetic youth ministry. Nevertheless, in order for this to occur, I suggest three movements. First, the youth ministry team must agree on the three interlocking commitments stated above. Second, identify the spiritual, personal and social needs of the youth in your target community or with your target group. Finally, intentionally program activities meeting the needs of these three areas. This simple model centered on Christ, guided by the power of the Holy Spirit and rooted in the principle of *transformation*, hopefully, will be a step toward developing more prophetic youth ministries (see fig. 1.2).

THE PROPHETIC URBAN CHRISTIAN YOUTH ARCHETYPE

At the beginning of this chapter, I identified three urban Christian youth archetypes. Each one, generally speaking, is associated with a particular

Table 1.2. Four Urban Christian Youth Archetypes. The section "Understanding of society" is greatly informed by H. Richard Niebuhr, *Christ and Culture* (New York: Harper Collins, 1951); Anthony Campolo and Donald Ratcliff, "Activist Youth Ministry," in Donald Ratcliff and James A. Davies, *Handbook of Youth Ministry* (Birmingham: Religious Education Press, 1991); Merton Strommen, Karen E. Jones and Dave Rahn, *Youth Ministry That Transforms* (Grand Rapids: Zondervan, 2001).

	Youth ministry paradigm	Theological persuasion	Role of youth worker	Understanding of Jesus	Understanding of Scripture	Understanding of self	Understanding of society
Dogmatic Christian youth	Traditional youth ministry	Conservative	Pastor	Jesus Christ is Lord and Savior	Reads Scripture through a tradition-specific interpretive lens (Evangelical, Pentecostal, Charismatic, Baptist, Orthodox, Catholic, etc.)	Dualistic: body/soul—flesh/spirit	Views culture as irredeemable; most countercultural. Society is at odds and incompatible with Christianity; one must affirm faith at the expense of culture.
Intellectual Christian youth	Liberal Youth Ministry	Liberal	Friend	Jesus is a good person and a wise sage	Reads the Scriptures metaphorically	Ethical: contributor to humanity; reason; potential	Overindulges culture; elevates society and complies with or accepts culture's moral and ethical values.
Socially engaged Christian youth	Activist youth ministry	Social gospel	Advocate	Jesus is a radical social activist	Reads the Scriptures from a social-justice perspective	Radical: structural and systemic change agent	Tends to have a "negative" perspective of culture. It is suspicious of society, which is in need of revolutionary change; society is sick, but change is possible with active engagement.
Prophetic youth	Prophetic youth ministry	Prophetic	Mentor and guide	Jesus as the liberator of spiritual, personal and social bondage and oppression	Reads the Scripture authoritatively and liberationally	Holistic: spiritual (heart), emotional (soul), physical (strength), intellectual (mind), social (neighbor), and moral (self) Luke 10:27	Tends to have a "positive" perspective of culture; views culture as redeemable. This youth ministry not only engages in projects and programs that impact communities and culture, but cultivates a transformational spirit and ethos along with evangelism. The liberating power of Jesus can transform any cultural construct.

youth ministry paradigm. The traditional youth ministry tends to foster dogmatic Christian youth. The liberal youth ministry tends to nurture intellectual Christian youth. The activist youth ministry tends to produce socially engaged Christian youth.

The fourth archetype is the prophetic urban Christian youth archetype. Prophetic Christian youth view Jesus as the liberator of spiritual, personal and social sin and oppression. First, prophetic Christian youth have a traditional understanding of the Holy Bible and Christian orthodoxy. They desire to grow and deepen their relationships with Jesus Christ. Second, they have a holistic understanding of the human person. They desire a healthy integration and development in the spiritual, personal and social realms of their lives. Finally, they believe in and are passionately committed to social justice.

Nicole is the youth worker at a theologically prophetic church. She is committed to holistic transformation of youth and their communities, fostering a balance of Christ-centered spiritual formation, personal development and a social-justice ethic. Hence, her lessons and programs address all three of these areas. She sees herself as mentor and guide for the youth. For Nicole, the primary goal of youth ministry is to nurture holistic youth who are growing in the Lord, in potential and in service.

Each paradigm offers a unique contribution to the field of youth ministry. I believe the prophetic youth ministry paradigm is the most effective and contextually relevant paradigm toward the transformation of urban youth and their communities. It is faithful to the Christian faith, encourages a holistic worldview and challenges youth ministries to be engaged in community development—meeting the spiritual, personal and social needs of youth. It honors Christ and urban communities.

2

Assumptions of a Prophetic Youth Ministry

The field of North American youth ministry is filled with assumptions which seem disconnected to the inner-city urban reality. For example, the current hot topics of postmodernism, technology and the emerging church, while certainly important, are rarely, if ever, examined to determine how they affect or influence urban youth ministries.

Resources for youth ministry are by and large conceived and produced outside the city. Consequently, cultural distinctives of the city often go unconsidered in those resources. So, for example, published youth ministry resources presume access to the Internet, even though only 36.7 percent of households making $20,000 to $29,999 (a range that includes the average household income in the South Bronx) have Internet access.[1] Youth ministry in the South Bronx does not benefit from the use of the Internet promoted in published youth ministry resources. It is not adequately equipped with those resources to address the challenges that South Bronx teens face in becoming competitive in the computer-dependent job market they will enter as adults. The urban youth worker must reasonably assume that most teens in the youth ministry, perhaps the overwhelming majority, do *not* have a computer or regular Internet

---

[1]"Presence of a Computer and the Internet for Households, by Selected Characteristics: September 2001," U.S. Census Bureau <http://www.census.gov/population/socdemo/computer/ppl-175/tab01A.pdf >. The average household income in the South Bronx is $20,809. It is a nearly impossible task to raise a family in New York City on this amount of income. In addition, according to the U.S. Census Bureau, 87 percent of households with an annual income of $75,000 or more have Internet access. Therefore, based on these figures, fewer than four out of ten South Bronx residents have Internet access.

access. Here we see the intersection of the postmodern age with social injustice.

COMPARING URBAN AND RURAL YOUTH MINISTRY

It may seem strange to include a section regarding rural youth ministry. Yet, I believe the following comparison might be interesting in light of the social dimension of prophetic youth ministry. Let me say from the outset that I have never been involved in rural ministry. Nor do I have any expertise in the area of rural youth ministry. However, based on a purely demographic analysis, one can infer certain similarities between urban youth ministry and rural youth ministry vis-à-vis middle-class or suburban youth ministry.

Questions to Ponder

While youth ministry resources encourage us to maximize Web potential, how can youth ministries overcome the lack of Internet access in inner-city youth ministries? How might the field of youth ministry examine this issue? How might middle-class youth workers partner with their inner-city counterparts to address, or at least assist with some of these issues?

If one examines the top twenty poorest congressional districts in the United States, the overwhelming majority of them represent inner-city urban and rural settings. Racially and ethnically speaking, most poor people in the inner-city urban context seem to be Latinos and African Americans. In rural settings, poverty tends to be more diverse and include many more poor whites. Nevertheless, this seems to highlight an interesting significant common ground: inner-city urban youth ministries and rural youth ministries tend to serve populations who are poorer and marginalized.

Conversely, if one examines the top twenty richest congressional districts in the United States, the overwhelming majority of them represent suburban and middle-class urban settings. Any standard census or demographic profile will show that these wealthier communities are not heavily populated by Latinos and African Americans.

This underscores the differences and realities between inner-city urban youth ministry and middle-class urban youth ministry. While they may share a common metropolis, they each experience a different real-

Table 2.1. Twenty Districts with the Lowest Median Household Income Among Congressional Districts (based on U.S. Census 2000, 108th congressional district summary data). "Poorest Congressional Districts," provided by Proximity, <www.proximityone.com/cd.htm>.

Rank	Congressional district	Median household income
1	Puerto Rico	$14,412
2	New York 16	$19,311
3	Kentucky 05	$21,915
4	West Virginia 03	$25,630
5	California 31	$26,093
6	Alabama 07	$26,672
7	California 20	$26,800
8	Mississippi 02	$26,894
9	Louisiana 05	$27,453
10	Louisiana 02	$27,514
11	Texas 15	$27,530
12	Missouri 08	$27,865
13	Oklahoma 02	$27,885
14	New York 15	$27,934
15	Pennsylvania 01	$28,295
16	North Carolina 01	$28,410
17	Arkansas 01	$28,940
18	South Carolina 06	$28,967
19	Texas 28	$29,127
20	New York 12	$29,195

ity and require a distinct ministry paradigm.

Based on economic realities, it is my supposition that most prophetic youth ministries will blossom in inner-city and poor rural areas. These youth ministries will reflect the spirit of youth seeking liberation from spiritual and social struggles.

URBAN YOUTH MINISTRY ASSUMPTIONS: AN HONEST SELF-EVALUATION

It is only fair that I address the equally unhelpful and frustrating urban youth ministry assumptions. These perspectives are based on the youth worker archetypes identified in chapter one.

The first urban youth worker perspective which frustrates me has overtly spiritual-eschatological assumptions. Workers with this perspective seem militantly concerned with the spiritual state of youth, yet oblivious to the realities of the teenagers' social and economic conditions. I am obviously concerned with the spiritual state of Christians. However, it seems disconnected, and, quite frankly, rather unloving, when youth workers seem so overwhelmingly focused on altar calls, faith commitments, enrollment in Christian religious education programs or moral behavior, without having the same concern for the teenagers' truancy issues, abuse at home, poverty, gang involvement and other challenges.

A casual reading of the Gospels shows Jesus' overwhelming compassion for and preferential treatment of the poor, marginalized outcasts, lepers, sinners, despised and women. How is it possible that youth workers ministering in a social and economic context not too dissimilar to that of the suffering Jews in first-century Israel can separate the social realities of teens from their spiritual concerns?

The second urban youth worker perspective which frustrates me is the touchy-feely type. Workers with this perspective exhibit overtly personal sympathetic and therapeutic assumptions which appear concerned about urban teens, but neither adequately challenge teens to grow in Christ nor attempt to address the hard-core justice issues of real-life blood-and-guts incarnation ministry. These tend to be either mainline youth workers or youth workers relocated from another setting who feel called to inner-city urban ministry.

Not all urban teens are at-risk youth or exhibit at-risk behavior—another popular assumption. Yet, based on the social and economic realities, an overwhelming number tend to live in at-risk situations. These situations include environments of poverty, violence, poor public schools, overpopulation and materialism. Inner-city teens need a gospel that can penetrate this reality. A soft Jesus and a wishy-washy gospel will never make it on the sidewalks of the city.

The third urban youth worker perspective which frustrates me has an overtly social-political assumption. These workers consider Jesus a homeboy in the struggle to turn over the political establishment. They tend to be more comfortable addressing social issues than proclaiming the gospel message. They attack the political establishment yet tend to become very comfortable with politicians who agree with their social justice stances, even at the expense of compromising significant moral issues.

While we must certainly stand with teens in their struggle for justice, our struggle is for a biblical justice and the expansion of the kingdom of God, not a social justice which is not Christ centered or promotes issues which contradict the Bible. Subverting the kingdom of man with the gospel message is one thing, but subverting the gospel message in the process is, quite frankly, not Christian.

ASSUMPTIONS OF A PROPHETIC YOUTH MINISTRY

Assumption one: Prophetic youth ministries assume that middle-class and suburban youth are not morally superior or less vulnerable to systemic evil than urban youth. Sin and redemption are transcultural and transeconomical. All people are in need of the saving power of Jesus Christ. While, theoretically speaking, those in the field may believe this, in actuality, I wonder if they really do. For example, why is it that middle-class and suburban youth ministries take mission trips to the inner city and not the other way around?

I welcome well-meaning Christian groups that create prayer stations in urban areas and presumably believe the city is in need of a special kind of outreach. I simply wonder if middle-class and suburban communities would welcome a bus load of black and Hispanic young people establishing prayer stations and praying for middle-class people and suburbanites?

Prophetic youth workers find these assumptions presumptuous at the least and colonialistic at worst. A prophetic youth ministry recognizes the sinfulness and righteousness of all people, regardless of culture, ethnicity, race, economics or gender.

Assumption two: Prophetic youth ministries assume social-justice engagement. A youth ministry that is prophetic is charitable, but a youth ministry that is charitable is not necessarily prophetic. The popular maxim comes to mind, "Give a person a fish, and the person eats for a day [charity]. Teach a person how to fish, and the person eats for a lifetime [justice]."

Prophetic youth ministries *must* be involved in social-justice reflection and action. A youth ministry *not* engaged in social justice is not prophetic. Prophetic youth ministries challenge their youth to examine social and systemic sin, as well as personal/spiritual sin. As Christians, we should believe that Jesus can liberate creation from all bondage—spiritual, personal and social. A Christian spirituality that addresses spiritual/personal sin at the exclusion of systemic and social sin is not a spirituality of liberation. This spirituality emphasizes the divinity of Christ at the expense of his humanity. Therefore, a youth ministry that addresses spiritual/person sin at the expense of systemic and social sin is not a prophetic youth ministry.

Assumption three: Prophetic youth ministries do not romanticize urban ministry. As urban ministers already know, there is nothing romantic about living in a situation of captivity. It is painful and ugly work. A prophetic youth worker is involved in the everyday struggles of urban families and the lives of teenagers outside the safe walls of the church. While salvation certainly transforms a young person's life, it does not necessarily make it any easier. Ask a gang member who has accepted Jesus what happens when he wants to leave the gang. Ask the pregnant teen who answers an altar call and wants to keep her baby while her uncaring, unbelieving boyfriend pressures her for an abortion. Ask the teenager who dropped out, is illiterate and can't read the Bible. Ask the urban youth worker who has little parental involvement in the ministry, no church funding, no private space for teens and no office in which to work, and is trying to develop the youth ministry when the church consists of thirty to forty members who are primarily elderly.

While middle-class and suburban families surely struggle with their own unique issues, at the end of the day, teens in middle-class or suburban settings, generally speaking, usually return to relatively stable neighborhoods and schools. This is often not the case in the inner city. Unfortunately, many urban teens do not have particularly stable neighborhoods or schools. Hence, the youth ministry may be the primary environment of empowerment and affirmation in the lives of urban teens and their families.

I thank God for my non-urban sisters and brothers who desire to work in the inner city. In my experience the ones who are able to minister successfully do not romanticize urban ministry. Through the everyday struggles of incarnational ministry, they earn the trust and respect of the community.

Assumption four: Prophetic youth workers have no racial, gender or denominational distinctives. God can and does call anyone to be a prophetic voice in the lives of youth regardless of race, gender or denominational tradition. I have met prophetic youth workers who are Latino, African American, Asian and white. I have interacted with male and female prophetic youth workers. I have seen prophetic youth ministries that are Pentecostal, evangelical and Roman Catholic.

As mentioned in chapter one, there are three commitments to prophetic youth ministry: (1) a commitment to the traditional understanding of the Holy Bible and Christian orthodoxy; (2) a commitment to the spiritual, personal and emotional development of youth; and (3) a commitment to social justice. While cultural assumptions can certainly impede effective dialogue and ministry, cultural distinctiveness does not.

Assumption five: Most youth ministries are not prophetic youth ministries. As mentioned in chapter one, based on my experience, most youth ministries in the urban context, particularly evangelical, Pentecostal and Roman Catholic youth ministries, seem to fall into the traditional youth ministry paradigm as part of their denominational tradition. While they are genuinely concerned about the spiritual lives of urban youth, they tend not to sufficiently engage in social-justice matters.

Assumptions can be a dangerous thing. When acknowledged, critically examined and processed, however, they can give helpful perspective and theoretical grounding.

3

The Holistic Approach

If a youth ministry implements the prophetic youth ministry model, it will automatically expand its boundaries. Nevertheless, the prophetic youth ministry model must be contextualized. What works in a Latino Pentecostal congregation may not work in an African American Baptist congregation or in an Asian Presbyterian congregation. Also, the prophetic youth ministry model is *not* intended to present or endorse a specific program or curriculum, which can be changed and adapted when necessary. It *is* intended to be understood as an overall youth ministry template toward creating a more holistic environment.

THE PROPHETIC YOUTH MINISTRY MODEL

The prophetic youth ministry is a biblically based model which flows from a conversation between Jesus and an expert on the Hebrew law.

> On one occasion an expert in the law stood up to test Jesus. "Teacher," he asked, "what must I do to inherit eternal life?"
>
> "What is written in the Law?" he replied. "How do you read it?"
>
> He answered: " 'Love the Lord your God with all your *heart* and with all your *soul* and with all your *strength* and with all your *mind*'; and, 'Love your *neighbor* as *yourself*.' "
>
> "You have answered correctly," Jesus replied. "Do this and you will live." (Luke 10:25-28, emphasis added)

In discussing the components necessary for inheriting eternal life, the expert identifies six areas, which Jesus affirms. The prophetic youth ministry model is rooted in these six areas: (1) the heart, (2) the soul, (3) the strength, (4) the mind, (5) the neighbor and (6) the self.[1]

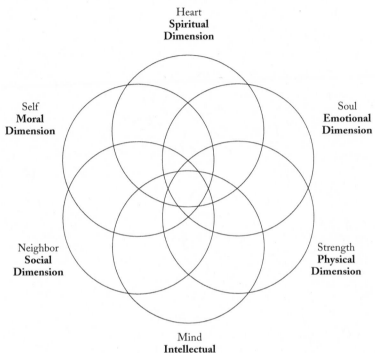

Areas	Needs of Urban Youth	Possible Programs
Heart	Spiritual	Bible study, retreats, spiritual disciplines, prayer services
Soul	Emotional	Support groups, mentoring programs, guest speakers, rap sessions
Strength	Physical	Sports tournaments, gym nights, nutrition lessons, health fairs
Mind	Intellectual	Tutoring, homework help, academic empowerment classes
Neighbor	Social	Service projects, food pantry, trips, college visits
Self	Moral	Sessions on moral living, healthy sexuality, relationships, etiquette

Figure 3.1. The holistic approach to prophetic youth ministry

[1]I am greatly indebted to the Reverend Roberto Rivera for this insight. Rivera, a respected pastor and family therapist, shared this framework in a chapel service at the Latino Pastoral Action Center located in the Bronx, New York. Since then, I have used this model personally, pedagogically and pastorally. I have adapted and further developed this framework into a holistic approach for the prophetic youth ministry paradigm.

THE HEART—NURTURING THE SPIRITUAL NEEDS OF URBAN YOUTH

Loving God with your heart means meeting the *spiritual* needs of urban youth and developing programming that addresses these needs. Most youth ministries address these needs. Unfortunately, this is also where they tend to stop.

As the word implies, this truly is the heart of the youth ministry—to grow in faith in Jesus Christ. However, the spiritual area is only one component of the human person. I believe that many teens and young adults *do not* attend youth ministries or eventually leave the church once they are old enough to do so because most churches tend to overemphasize the spiritual aspects of their ministry so that they seem disconnected or disinterested with the other areas of the lives of urban youth. In order to be more effective in the urban context, youth ministries must shift from a spiritual-services-only ministry to a multiservices ministry. This will move the youth ministry toward a more holistic approach—meeting the full needs of urban youth. This is what liberal and activist youth ministries do very well.

Possible programming. To nurture sprititual development, a youth worker can plan activities such as Bible study, retreats, teaching youth how to develop spiritual disciplines, lessons on early church history and prayer services.

Questions to Ponder

The prophetic youth ministry fosters a spiritually healthy environment. Does your youth ministry foster a spiritually healthy environment? If not, why not? What are the obstacles? What can your leadership team do to create a healthier spiritual environment which glorifies God? Are your youth worker and youth ministry leadership team spiritually healthy?

THE SOUL—NURTURING THE EMOTIONAL NEEDS OF URBAN YOUTH

Loving God with your soul means meeting the *emotional* needs of urban youth and developing programming that addresses these needs. As previously mentioned, youth ministries should be careful not to overspiritualize youth problems or issues. The adolescent years are challenging and emotionally stressful. This is the time of identity exploration, hormonal changes and developmental growth. Furthermore, recent brain research, as will be examined later, shows that ongoing mental development influences teen behavior. Program activities should also address the emotional needs of urban youth.

When teens are experiencing difficulties, we must be careful not to demonize their behavior, requiring of them simply more prayer or greater church attendance. Perhaps what is needed is programming that allows teens to explore and address emotional issues in a healthy Christian environment. Here lies the rub: if urban youth are experiencing emotional challenges *and* if the church does not provide a safe, nonjudgmental environment to help them process these issues and questions, they will undoubtedly go somewhere else for help. Unfortunately, these persons or places—gangs, nightclubs and the street—may not necessarily share the values of the church.

Possible programming. Prophet youth ministries can offer support groups, develop mentoring programs, invite guest speakers to address adolescent-appropriate issues (depression, suicide, peer pressure) and facilitate rap sessions on teen-selected issues.

THE STRENGTH—NURTURING THE PHYSICAL NEEDS OF URBAN YOUTH

Loving God with your strength means meeting the *physical/bodily* needs of urban youth and developing programming that addresses these needs. There is probably no easier way to attract urban youth, especially boys, to church than to offers sports, recreation and fitness programs.

Questions to Ponder

The prophetic youth ministry fosters an emotionally healthy environment. Does your youth ministry foster an emotionally healthy environment? If not, why not? What are the obstacles? What can your leadership team do to create a healthier emotional environment which glorifies God? Are your youth worker and youth ministry leadership team emotionally healthy?

A youth ministry that offers physical activities will address at least five areas. First, in urban communities with scarce resources, this will provide a wholesome environment for healthy physical exercise and play. Second, it shows the community that the church/youth ministry cares about the neighborhood and wants to be actively involved in the lives of local youth. Third, it provides greatly needed health and body education. Fourth, this is a great way to nurture relationship/friendship evangelism. Teens may not attend church, but they will attend a church-sponsored sports event. The church can have a table with free water and information about the youth ministry. Finally, addressing the physical/bodily needs of urban youth begins to overcome the Christian tendency to condemn the body and flesh and develop a healthier and more holistic perspective of seeing the body as a temple of the Holy Spirit, which needs exercise, care and affection.

Questions to Ponder

The prophetic youth ministry fosters a physically healthy environment. Does your youth ministry foster a physically healthy environment? If not, why not? What are the obstacles? What can your leadership team do to create a healthier physical environment which glorifies God? Are your youth worker and youth ministry leadership team physically/bodily healthy?

Possible programming. A youth ministry can sponsor sports tournaments, host open gym nights or late-night bowling nights, invite nutritionists to teach health sessions, sponsor health fairs, and provide fitness and nutrition classes.

THE MIND—NURTURING THE INTELLECTUAL NEEDS OF URBAN YOUTH

Loving God with your mind means meeting the *intellectual/academic* needs of urban youth and developing programming that addresses these needs. In addition to addressing the previously mentioned emotional and physical needs, a prophetic youth ministry must also confront the academic and learning challenges of many of our youth in the urban context.

Any standard demographic evaluation of inner-city communities in the United States highlights the staggering drop-out rates of urban teens. The numbers of minorities attending colleges, while increasing, are scandalously low.[2] And, of course, as the world becomes more technologically sophisticated, the unemployment and underemployment rates remain a

---

[2]See American Council on Education, Center for Advancement of Racial and Ethnic Equality, *Reflections on 20 Years of Minorities in Higher Education and the Annual ACE Status Report* (Washington, DC: ACE, 2004) <www.acenet.edu/Content/NavigationMenu/ProgramsServices/CAREE/2004_reflections_msr.pdf>.

painful reality. Sadly, there also seems to be, in my experience, a general sense among many urban youth that education is optional, incorrect grammar is acceptable, foul language is appropriate, obtaining a GED is the same as receiving a high school diploma, and higher learning is either unattainable, unaffordable or unnecessary.

I do not deny the massive obstacles that confront urban youth, such as discrimination, poverty, violence, disinterested teachers and subpar schools. Nevertheless, I wish to emphasize that prophetic youth ministries *must* address the intellectual and academic needs of urban youth.

Possible programming. Unfortunately, churches and youth ministries in the inner city cannot assume that teens are receiving a proper education in public schools. Urban youth ministries can be creative in meeting this need. For example, a youth ministry can offer a tutoring and homework-help program two or three days per week, hire a teacher to facilitate an academic empowerment class, develop an adult volunteer team, or purchase a student learning curriculum from educational publications such as McGraw-Hill, Houghton Mifflin, or Pearson and offer a ten-week class to the entire community. A church can simply open its doors and allow teens a safe and quiet place to read and study. A church could even partner with a school or teaching program and offer the church space as a host site. There are so many excellent curricula already developed. All you need is a lead person with a heart for learning and urban youth to teach the class.

Questions to Ponder

The Prophetic Youth Ministry fosters an intellectually healthy environment. Does your youth ministry foster an intellectually healthy environment? Does it encourage higher education? If not, why not? What are the obstacles? What can your leadership team do to create a healthier intellectual environment which glorifies God? Are your youth worker and youth ministry leadership team intellectually healthy?

THE NEIGHBOR—NURTURING THE SOCIAL NEEDS OF YOUTH

Loving your neighbor means meeting the *social* (interrelational) needs of urban youth and developing programming that addresses these needs. This can be addressed in two ways: social service activities and recreational activities.

There is little more spiritually and emotionally healthy than service. Helping urban youth to love their neighbor is an excellent way to instill in them a sense of civic duty and social justice. Developmentally, it balances the natural ego-centered perspective of adolescence. Service projects are also an educational experience. They help teens and youth ministries to reach out beyond themselves. For example, providing food to those in need teaches about the dynamics of poverty, economics, and power structures and develops a compassionate ethos.

Meeting the social needs should also include healthy and fun activities. This may include going to movies, hanging out at the home of one of the parishioners or attending a professional sporting event.

An underutilized, inexpensive and fun activity is attending a local college sporting event. These intercollegiate games are intense and exciting. The most popular sports tend to be football games and men's basketball games. Sometimes fees are required for these two men's sporting events, but you can request complementary tickets from the athletics department. However, almost all other sports are free, such as women's basketball, men's baseball, women's softball, swimming, wrestling, tennis, golf, rowing, squash, track and field, volleyball, water polo, and cheerleading.

Also, if youth workers contact the coach or team captain, he or she might recruit some of the players to meet with the youth group. College players are just a few years older than teens. Yet, from the adolescent perspective, college students are often bigger than life and can serve as inspirational role models. Of course, this also serves as a way to bring urban youth onto a college campus.

Meeting the social needs of youth is vital. Both serious service projects and casual recreational activities help to develop deeper bonds of friendship and fellowship. These are also excellent opportunities for youth workers to connect with their teens outside the church environment.

Possible programming. Service projects may include developing a food pantry, providing various social service projects, cleaning the neighborhood, painting over graffiti-covered walls or facilitating a community-needs assessment to identify which needs should receive the program's focus. For casual social activities, the church could host trips to amusement parks or professional or collegiate sporting events, perhaps partnering with other youth ministries.

THE SELF—NURTURING THE MORAL NEEDS OF YOUTH

Loving yourself means addressing the *moral* (intrarelational) needs of urban youth and developing programming that addresses these moral (intrarelational) needs. As Christians, we tend to interchange our understanding of the body or the flesh (physical) with morality (moral).

Without overtheologizing, the body is a wonderful thing. God became flesh in the body. If the body or flesh were bad, God would certainly not have become enfleshed in Jesus Christ. Furthermore, when we say "your body is a temple of the Holy Spirit" or "you are not your own" (1 Corinthians 6:19), we are expressing a virtuous attitude toward the human body.

The natural desires of the body are, in and of themselves, amoral, but obsession with these desires may lead to immorality. Let us examine the traditional seven deadly sins (see table 3.1).

Questions to Ponder

The prophetic youth ministry fosters a socially healthy environment. Does your youth ministry foster a socially healthy environment? If not, why not? What are the obstacles? What can your leadership team do to create a healthier social environment which glorifies God? Are your youth worker and youth ministry leadership team socially/relationally healthy?

Table 3.1. Seven Deadly Sins and Seven Virtues

Sins	Virtues
Pride	Dedication, hard work
Gluttony	Temperance, moderation, abstinence
Lust	Self-control, chastity
Wrath/anger	Kindness, patience
Greed	Generosity, simplicity
Envy	Humility, love
Sloth	Zeal, diligence

Experiencing dedication, hard work and the satisfaction of a job well done is a good thing; becoming prideful is immoral. Admiring and celebrating the works of others is a joyful experience; becoming envious is immoral. The virtues which counter envy are humility and love. Enjoying tasty foods and eating snacks is fine; becoming gluttonous is immoral. The virtues which counter gluttony are temperance, moderation and abstinence. Attraction to the opposite gender is healthy, and enjoying the intimacy of one's spouse is a great thing; becoming lustful is immoral. The virtues which counter lust are self-control and chastity. Righteous anger against an injustice is appropriate; becoming revengefully angry is immoral. The virtues which counter wrath or anger are kindness and patience. Wanting a good, blessed and financially secure life for yourself and your family is desirable; becoming greedy or covetous is immoral. The virtues which counter greed are generosity and simplicity. Finally, wanting time to rest, rejuvenate and avoid workaholism is necessary; becoming slothful is immoral. The virtues which counter sloth are zeal, enthusiasm and diligence.[3]

Questions to Ponder

The prophetic youth ministry fosters a morally healthy environment. Does your youth ministry foster such an environment? If not, why not? What are the obstacles? What can your leadership team do to create a healthier moral environment which glorifies God? Are your youth worker and youth ministry leadership team morally healthy?

In addressing the physical needs of urban youth, we are expressing a *positive* perspective of the body. In addressing the moral needs of urban youth, we now move toward an understanding of moral behavior. This distinction is vital. On the one hand, we want to develop in youth a healthy attitude about their bodies. On the other hand, we also want them to know that Christian morality is a lifestyle and worldview. For example, a person can be sexually pure, yet live a sinful life. Being honest with people is moral behavior. Respecting people's property is moral behavior. And, of course, liv-

---

[3]This section was informed by "7 Deadly Sins," 7 Deadly Sins.com <http://deadlysins.com/sins/index.htm>, and "The Seven Deadly Sins," *The Whitestone Journal*, June 18, 1996 (updated August 27, 2004) <http://www.whitestonejournal.com/seven>.

ing a healthy Christian sexual lifestyle is moral behavior.

Unlike loving the neighbor, which reflects the social needs of youth, loving the self reflects the importance of taking care of one's self. This nurtures for youth a healthier and more holistic appreciation of themselves.

Four Bible passages can serve as significant guides in developing the moral component of the prophetic youth ministry: (1) the Golden Rule (Luke 6:31), (2) the Beatitudes (Matthew 5:1-12), (3) Life by the Spirit (Galatians 5:16-25), and (4) the Ten Commandments (Exodus 20:1-21).

Possible programming. To nurture healthy self-loving youth, a church can offer sessions on moral living and developing healthy sexuality and relationships; etiquette classes; retreats; and "days of spiritual/personal style" for girls and for boys.

Table 3.2. Implementing the Holistic Approach to Prophetic Youth Ministry

Areas	Needs of urban youth	Possible programs
Heart	Spiritual	Bible study, retreats, spiritual disciplines, prayer services
Soul	Emotional	Support groups, mentoring programs, guest speakers, rap sessions
Strength	Physical	Sports tournaments, gym nights, nutrition lessons, health fairs
Mind	Intellectual	Tutoring, homework help, academic empowerment classes
Neighbor	Social	Service projects such as food pantry, trips, college visits
Self	Moral	Sessions on moral living, healthy sexuality, relationships, etiquette

Table 3.3. A Model for Spiritual Formation

The six areas of the human person	The needs which are addressed	Reflective questions
Heart	Spiritual	Am I developing my devotional habits?
Soul	Emotional	Am I maturing emotionally?
Strength	Physical	Am I taking care of my body?
Mind	Intellectual	Am I continuing to learn and study new things?
Neighbor	Social (interpersonal)	Am I reaching out to others, especially the poor and marginalized?
Self	Moral (intrapersonal)	Am I living a moral lifestyle?

4

Leading Youth

A REFLECTION-ACTION PRAXIS

Prophetic youth ministry in the urban context requires spiritual, personal and social reflection-action exegesis. First, youth are invited to delve into the Scriptures to better understand and hear what God's Word is saying to them (spiritual). Second, they are encouraged to apply its principles in a real and practical way (personal). Finally, for urban youth to truly appreciate these biblical teachings, they must be relevant to, interact with and transform the urban context (social).

The methodology I am proposing falls within the critical-theory or radical-education school of pedagogy identified as reflection-action praxis. It is helpful to read Bruce Jackson's comments on praxis.

> A distinction should be made between praxis and practice. Practice of ministry is the doing of things as they relate to ministry. Things such as preaching, counseling, community organizing, and administration contain elements of ministerial practice or functioning. Praxis involves the doing of these skills, but it also adds theological reflection upon what is being done, why it is done, how it is done, and what could be done. It marries action (doing) with reflection (being). The action must seek to transform the world, and theological reflection must be done to understand and shape the acting process. The problem many of us face is that we often emphasize one at the expense of the other.[1]

The five-movement reflection-action praxis can be used for Bible study

---

[1]Eldin Villafañe, Douglas Hall, Efrain Agosto and Bruce W. Jackson, *Seek the Peace of the City: Reflections on Urban Ministry* (Grand Rapids: Eerdmans, 1995), pp. 129-30.

with personal application *or* for social action. Either way, it intentionally considers the context of the urban setting. The praxis utilizes the Socratic method, that is, a process of seeking truth through intentional dialogue and a progression of questions. This encourages and challenges youth to wrestle with the issue and seek the answer for themselves, instead of simply giving them an answer. The five components include (1) experience, (2) examination, (3) reflection, (4) action and (5) evaluation.[2]

MOVEMENT ONE: EXPERIENCE

The purpose of the first movement is to help youth to reflect and express their thoughts about a presenting issue as it relates to their present personal experiences. This begins and grounds the process in the present moment and the personal context of their real-life experiences. Since this action begins with youth, the primary objects of reflection are youth themselves.

During this first movement, it is important for the members of the youth group to share a *personal* statement about the present issue and not a theoretical statement. For example, a helpful question to lead the discussion would be, What does leadership mean to you? This non-threatening question invites them to reflect on the issue in a way that is personal and self-reflective.

An unhelpful question would be, What is leadership? This second question is too broad and overly theoretical. Because it requires a formal right or wrong definition, it will tend to silence the discussion.

A follow-up question might be, How did you come to this understanding of leadership? This invites teens to examine their answers and express how they came to this understanding.

These examples highlight the importance of thoughtful questions. A well-prepared facilitator will plan open-ended questions in advance. Close-ended questions, those requiring a simple yes or no answer or a single-word response, will stop the flow of discussion. Furthermore, questions which require a textbook type of answer will make youth feel more like they are taking a school exam rather than examining a biblical principle and how it applies to their lives.

---

[2]This five-step methodology has been greatly informed by Thomas H. Groome, *Christian Religious Education: Sharing Our Story and Vision* (San Francisco: Jossey-Bass, 1980), and Paulo Freire, *Pedagogy of the Oppressed*, trans. Myra Bergman Ramos, 30th ed. (New York: Continuum, 2000).

MOVEMENT TWO: EXAMINATION

The purpose of the second movement is to gather and critically examine the information on the presenting issue or topic being addressed and to explore God's Word. This movement, however, goes beyond simply giving information or providing answers. Many urban youth have been miseducated or undereducated from both formal and informal sources of education. In *Lies My Teacher Told Me,* James Loewen takes special aim at the miseducation of minority youth in the subject of American history.

> High school students hate history. When they list their favorite subjects, history invariably comes last. . . . African American, Native American, and Latino students view history with a special dislike. They also learn history especially poorly. Students of color do only slightly worse than white students in mathematics. If you'll pardon my grammar, non-white students do more worse in English and most worse in history. Something intriguing is going on here: surely history is not more difficult for minorities than trigonometry or Faulkner. Students don't even know they are alienated, only that they "don't like social studies" or "aren't any good in history." College teachers in most disciplines are happy when their students have had significant exposure to the subject before college. Not teachers in history. History professors in college routinely put down high school history courses. A colleague of mine calls his survey of American history "Iconoclasm I and II," because he sees his job as disabusing his charges of what they learned in high school. . . . The way American history is taught particularly alienates students of color and children from impoverished families. . . . Arthur M. Schlesinger, Jr. denounces Afrocentrism as "psychotherapy" for blacks—a one-sided misguided attempt to make African Americans feel good about themselves. Unfortunately, the Eurocentric history in our textbooks amounts to psychotherapy for whites. . . . Surely we do not really want a generation of African Americans raised on anti-white Afrocentric history, but just as surely, we cannot afford another generation of white Americans raised on complacent celebratory Eurocentric history. . . . The message that Eurocentric history sends to non-European Americans is: your ancestors have not done much of importance.[3]

Therefore, this second movement serves as a deconstructing and recon-

---

[3]James W. Loewen, *Lies My Teacher Told Me: Everything Your American History Textbook Got Wrong* (New York: Touchstone; Simon and Schuster, 1995), pp. 12, 301, 302.

structing of the learning experience. While the whole process is educational, this second movement intentionally teaches and equips youth, through an interactive teacher-student dialectic, with the necessary tools and techniques needed for a more critical education. Teachers are encouraged to utilize various interactive activities, such as dialectical lectures, inventories, kinesthetic activities, visuals, storytelling, videos, music and other pedagogical methods.

In addition to examining other texts—whether academic, resource or life texts—the second movement critically examines God's Word and what it says about the respective issue or topic. This exegesis should be informational and applicable. The biblical hermeneutics of this lesson should certainly reinforce the theological lesson of the day, but it should also address the student's cultural hermeneutics, if it is to be relevant. Once the teacher has facilitated a discourse involving the student, the Bible and culture, it is time to move to the next movement.

MOVEMENT THREE: REFLECTION

The purpose of the third movement is to help youth self-reflect and hermeneutically interact with the presenting issue in light of the young person's experience, information examined and God's Word. This involves three aspects: (1) dialogue with self, (2) dialogue with God and (3) dialogue with others.

In Martin Buber's classic work, *I and Thou*, he views human relationships in two fundamentally different ways: I-It and I-Thou relationships.[4] The I-It relationship refers to the normal, everyday relationships of human beings with the things surrounding them. People may consider others It. In fact, he argues, this is what people do most of the time. People view others from a distance, like a thing, a part of the environment, forged into chains of causality.

The I-Thou relationship is radically different. The human being enters into the I-Thou relationship with his or her innermost and whole being. In this meeting, a real dialogue occurs. This relationship between the I and the Thou is one of mutuality, openness and directness—an authentic dialogue.

---

[4]Martin Buber, *I and Thou* (New York: Charles Scribner's Sons, 1970).

For Buber, the I-Thou relationship is a reflection of the human meeting with God. In fact, the ultimate objective is not only the I-Thou relationship between the person and the world, but the relationship between the person and God. God can be known through this subjective view of the universe. One can encounter God in the revelation of everyday existence. Buber argues that the essence of the biblical religion is the possibility that a dialogue between the human and God exists, regardless of the infinite abyss between them. Furthermore, Buber asserts, the Bible is a record of this dialogue experience between humans and God. He believes the essence of religious life is not the affirmation of religious beliefs, but the way in which one meets the challenges of existence.

This, of course, has significant spiritual, personal and social implications for urban youth. Based on the descriptions provided by Buber, many urban youth have been conditioned to view themselves, their relationships and their communities through an I-It perspective.

Dialogue with self. Following the examination component, youth are invited to quietly reflect on their new discoveries, a dialogue with the I. Some helpful questions in this movement may be, What new thing have you discovered about yourself? What insight did the teacher provide for you? What word, phrase or thought had an impact on you? Reflecting with the I allows the person time to process and digest the information. However, in an urban world filled with loudness and busyness, a brief moment for self-reflection may be challenging at first for a youth group, but it allows them space for self-reflection.

Dialogue with God. The participants are now invited to dialogue with God through his Word and quiet reflection, a dialogue with the "Great Thou." Here the teacher will briefly guide the teens through preselected Bible passages which intentionally address or speak of the present issue/topic.[5]

---

[5]Although there is some similarity, the dialogue with God component is *not* meant to describe or practice *lectio divina*, the classic method of meditating on God's Word. According to Luke Dysinger, *lectio divina* is "a slow, contemplative praying of the Scriptures which enables the Bible, the Word of God, to become a means of union with God." *Lectio divina* comprises four movements: (1) reading and listening to God's Word *(lectio)*, (2) meditation on the Scripture passage *(meditatio)*, (3) prayer with God *(oratio)*, and (4) contemplation or resting with God *(contemplatio)*. See Luke Dysinger, "Accepting the Embrace of God: The Ancient Art of *Lectio Divina*," *Valyermo Benedictine* 1, no. 1 (Spring 1990) <www.valyermo.com/ld-art.html>.

Again, this should be brief without giving away "answers." The teacher should simply nurture an environment conducive to conversation between youth and God, allowing them time to self-reflect. Some helpful questions might be, What word or phrase is God sharing with you in a personal way? What burden or passion is God placing on your heart as you read this passage and reflect on the present issue? What is God saying to you?

Dialogue with others. After a brief time, the participants gather in small groups and share with each other what they have discovered, a dialogue with Thou. Continuing with Buber's insight, the dialogue is not a time to talk back and forth, as the I-It conversation tends to be. Reflecting with the Thou requires two dynamics: sharing and listening. As one person talks, the others simply listen. The small group begins to share its stories in a nonjudgmental environment.

In *Pedagogy of the Oppressed*, Friere offers this insight regarding the transformative power of dialogue:

> Dialogue with people is radically necessary to every authentic revolution. This is what makes it a revolution, as distinguished from a military coup. One does not expect dialogue from a coup—only deceit or force. Sooner or later, a true revolution must initiate a courageous dialogue with the people. . . . The earlier dialogue begins, the more truly revolutionary will the movement be.[6]

Freire offers five requirements for authentic transformational dialogue. First, dialogue cannot exist in the absence of profound love. Second, dialogue requires humility. Third, dialogue requires an intense faith in the human person, to create and recreate. Fourth, dialogue requires hope, a hope that is aware of our incompleteness, but does not accept or settle for silence or escape. Finally, dialogue requires critical reflection.

For many of our teens, Bible-study sessions or Sunday school classes tend to include a great deal of talking by an adult leader and very little talking by youth. A safe, nonjudgmental space for authentic dialogue energizes the conversation, respects the reflections of youth and challenges them to think for themselves.

---

[6]Freire, *Pedagogy of the Oppressed,* p. 128.

"Break it down and keep it real"—a contextual hermeneutical dialectic.
Several years ago, after preaching to a group of two hundred teens in a
South Bronx gymnasium, I asked a teenager what he thought of my sermon. He paused a moment and said, "Fred, you gotta break it down and
keep it real man."

Break it down. Keep it real. Break it down—hermeneutic, exegesis and
everyday language. Keep it real—authenticity, solidarity and context. Un-
knowingly, this teenager gave us a template for a contextual hermeneutical
dialectic. He recognized that communication in and of itself (the sermon,
in this case), regardless of its good intentions, will not transform the listen-
ers unless there is an understanding of the people's experiences—the people's unique suffering. Even though the message I delivered may have connected well with one group of youth, it may not necessarily connect with a
different group. A contextual hermeneutical dialectic recognizes this dynamic.

Not all urban youth ministries are the same. A Latino Pentecostal
church is certainly different from a Latino Roman Catholic church. An
African American Pentecostal church is certainly different from an African American Baptist church. As previously addressed, contextualization
is the heart of urban youth ministry. It is the locus, the place where the
work takes place. Youth ministry is not an abstract theory or theology. It is
nothing less than the work of transformation incarnated within a very specific context. Contextualization is the place of the incarnation, where the
Word is enfleshed within a historical and experiential situation.

In *Galilean Journey*, Virgilio Elizondo expresses the significance of one's
context informing a developing theology and thought process.[7] As examined in chapter three, one's anthropology cannot be separated from one's
hermeneutic. This is the same for ministry. It would be like trying to understand Jesus without acknowledging his first-century Jewish culture. For
contextualization, this dichotomy is nonsensical.

Elizondo shares that he is a Mexican American Roman Catholic priest
who was born in the United States and grew up in San Antonio, Texas. It

---

[7]Virgilio Elizondo, *Galilean Journey: The Mexican-American Promise* (Maryknoll, N.Y.: Orbis, 1983),
pp. 1-2.

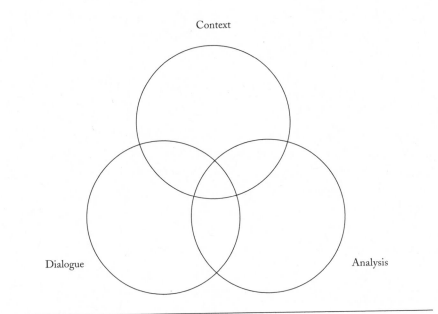

Context

Dialogue

Analysis

Figure 4.1. Contextual hermeneutical dialectic

is through this lens that he views life. He writes, "It is from this optic that I search for the truth that has shaped my life to this point, and will shape my future."[8] Contextualization gives theology hands.

The contextual hermeneutical dialectic in this reflection-action praxis, and particularly within the third movement, invites youth to critically reflect and interpret all texts—biblical texts and life texts—from the context of their local situation. What works in the South Bronx may not work in South Los Angeles or in South Boston. Prophetic youth ministry encourages and equips urban youth to apply a critical hermeneutic. Its applicability and relevance to its local demographic is dependent on their context.

While the classical theological dialectic understands theology objectively, the contextual theological dialectic understands theology subjectively. As Stephen Bevans writes, "We can certainly learn from others, but the theology of others can never be our own."[9] This is particularly significant within movement four: action. As youth develop a plan of action, they

---

[8]Ibid.
[9]Stephen B. Bevans, "Contextual Theology as a Theological Imperative," in *Models of Contextual Theology*, Faith and Cultures (Maryknoll, N.Y.: Orbis, 1992), p. 5.

may find that a specific transformative intervention in one context may not be appropriate or effective in another context. What *is* shared among all urban youth is the spirit of solidarity and the developing vision of hope during the process of the contextual hermeneutical dialectic.

MOVEMENT FOUR: ACTION

The purpose of movement four is to help youth to develop a strategic plan of action to address the presenting issue. This fourth movement is the pinnacle of the methodological process. It empowers youth to re-envision the future, move from reflection to action and begin to identify how they will live out their lives and influence their community differently. This is the process of transformation, the primary metaphor of the prophetic youth ministry. Helpful questions in this movement might be, Now that we have identified the presenting issue, reflected on God's Word, and discussed this with each other, what are we going to do? What are some specific ways we can address the issue?

Questions to Ponder

The reflection-action praxis provides a method of engaging youth in biblical study and community action. What model or approach does the youth ministry utilize to study Scripture? How effective is that model? How might the reflection-action process be implemented? How might it be received? Is the youth ministry engaged in community development? What community issues are directly affecting the teens? How might the reflection-action praxis help in processing and addressing these issues?

MOVEMENT FIVE: EVALUATION

The purpose of movement five is twofold: (1) to evaluate the results of the reflection-action praxis as it relates to the presenting issue and (2) to identify the next presenting issue to address. This final movement is actually occurring throughout the process. One is continuously evaluating and improving. However, more intentionally this phase formally evaluates the methodological praxis, particularly the action movement. Were the goals of the action plan met? What worked? What didn't work? What have we learned through this process? What next presenting issue should be addressed?

If the teacher is using this model as a

Bible-study method, the evaluation can be used to begin the following session. In other words, the teacher may begin class by briefly reviewing the previous session and then asking, How did you do with the action plan you developed last week? Were the goals you identified met during the week?[10]

UTILIZING THE REFLECTION-ACTION PRAXIS

Youth workers interested in the reflection-action praxis method may utilize this method in at least four different ways: (1) one-session model, (2) five-session model, (3) retreat model and (4) semester model.

One-session model. In this first model, the youth worker facilitates the method with his or her group within a single session. The following are two suggested outlines:

	Outline 1	Outline 2
Movement one: experience	10 minutes	5 minutes
Movement two: examination	10 minutes	10 minutes
Movement three: reflection	10 minutes	15 minutes
Movement four: action	10 minutes	20 minutes
Movement five: evaluation	10 minutes	5 minutes

Five-session model. In this second model, the youth worker facilitates the method with his or her group in five sessions, one movement per week.

Session one	Movement one: experience
Session two	Movement two: examination
Session three	Movement three: reflection
Session four	Movement four: action
Session five	Movement five: evaluation

Naturally, this allows for more in-depth examination of the presenting issue. Youth workers would also have more time to add various supplemental teaching activities or include guest speakers.

Retreat method. In this third model, the teacher facilitates the method with his or her group during the course of a weekend retreat. The following is a suggested outline:

---

[10]The development of questions in movement five was informed by the method provided in Lawrence O. Richards and Gary Bredfeldt, *Creative Bible Teaching,* rev. ed. (Chicago: Moody Press, 1998).

Friday night	Movement one: experience (with night prayer and fellowship)
Saturday	Prayer
	Breakfast
	Session one—Movement two: examination
	Session two—Movement three: reflection
	Lunch
	Afternoon of free time
	Dinner
	Movement four: action (with night prayer and fellowship)
Sunday morning	Breakfast
	Worship service
	Movement five: evaluation

This model is particularly effective if the retreat is a working retreat or leadership retreat that requires more intense dialogue along with greater time for planning. If this is the case, more time may be dedicated to movement three (reflection) and movement four (action). Furthermore, there could be a decrease in the Saturday free time and an increase in the reflection-action processing.

Semester model. In this fourth model, the teacher facilitates the method with his or her group during the course of an entire semester. The semester model follows the same format as the five-session model but expands the method throughout an entire semester: fall, spring or summer. The following is a suggested outline:

Weeks one to two	Movement one: experience
Weeks three to five	Movement two: examination (includes various learning formats, videos, trips or guest speakers)
Weeks six to eight	Movement three: reflection (includes small groups, prayer service or interactive activities)
Weeks nine to eleven	Movement four: action (includes planning and service projects)
Week twelve	Movement five: evaluation (includes final reflections, evaluations and closing ceremonies)

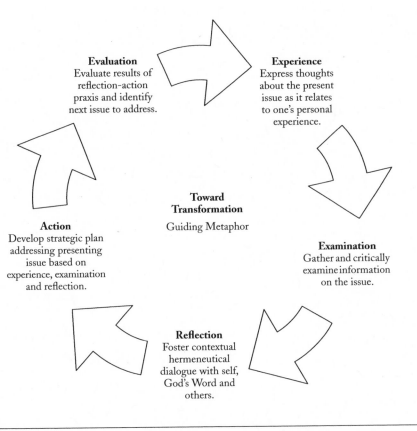

Figure 4.2. Reflection-action praxis for the prophetic youth ministry

Again, the semester model may be adapted as needed. This also allows the prophetic youth ministry the flexibility to develop its own indigenous curricula based on its contextual needs and realities.

REFLECTION-ACTION PRAXIS IN PRACTICE

I will now process two examples using the reflection-action praxis. The first examines a social issue that has an impact on youth. The second examines a more traditional spiritual issue: Communion.

Example one: A social issue affecting youth.
Movement one: experience. During this first stage, invite the youth to

more intentionally examine their community and experiences with a critical eye. Identify the felt needs of these teens. Pain and suffering are not abstract concepts. Many urban youth suffer from poverty, unemployment, racism, miseducation, violence and other challenges. This movement involves being present in the lives of urban youth within their context. It also names the injustice. To name an injustice is a defiant act establishing a radical posture of solidarity with those who struggle against oppression. Thus, the first movement is relational and incarnational. That is, the youth worker must become enfleshed among the youth. In movement one, I suggest as a primary question, What injustices and suffering are youth experiencing in this community?

Allow the young people to share their responses. After identifying and listing their experiences with injustice and suffering, select one which will serve as the presenting issue.

Movement two: examination. During this movement, the group engages in a more thoughtful and informed social analysis. It goes beyond the felt needs of the community to a more historical, demographical and social study of the issues. Root causes and their consequences are identified. In this discussion, the youth should analyze the structures of society, the way they interrelate and the underlying dynamic which governs them. Models and theories are reviewed and evaluated. More penetrating questions about root causes of systemic and structural injustice are asked. During this movement, the group begins to obtain a more complete picture of a situation by exploring historical, political and structural relationships. In movement two, I suggest three primary questions: What is the root cause of this injustice or suffering? Who are the people and structures in power that benefit from those who are suffering? Who are the specific people who are suffering?

Use a variety of methods to inform the group. After a more formal examination of the presenting issue and allowing time for the group to consider these questions, the group now moves to a more in-depth conversation.

Movement three: reflection. During this movement, the group integrates what has been learned through the social analysis of the previous movement within their specific faith tradition. The group evaluates the issues in a more reflective way—intellectually and spiritually—in light of the

Scriptures, the teachings of the church and the specific traditions of the congregation's faith. It is during this movement that the youth group begins to envision hope in addressing the presenting issue. In movement three, I suggest two primary questions: What do we hope and envision will happen in regards to this issue? What are we, as a youth ministry and congregation, committed to doing?

First, the youth are given time to dialogue with the self. They can journal, draw pictures, write a poem, consider a song or simply reflect quietly. Next, the youth dialogue with God. Provide specific Scripture passages or church teaching which addresses the issue. Invite the students to respond to God's Word. What does God's Word say about this issue? How do you connect the issue with God's Word? Finally, the youth dialogue with each other. They are invited to share their thoughts and insights. This is not a time for debate but a time of sharing and listening. After these dialogues, it is time for planning and action.

Movement four: action. Action does not bring an end to the process. Unfortunately, there will always be another injustice and suffering which needs to be addressed. A prophetic youth ministry envisions community transformation, but for a transformative vision to become actualized, it requires education, reflection and action. During this fourth movement, the group develops and tests strategies which enable transformation to evolve. A planned response is prepared and put into action. Transformation is both a theory and a planned process. In movement four, I suggest these primary questions: What is our plan of action to address this issue? What specific strategies should we employ?

The youth are now more informed about the presenting issue based on their own experiences (movement one), recent examination (movement two) and critical reflection (movement three). Now, they begin to write down a strategic plan of action to address the issue. It is important to help the group develop a realistic plan. The notion that an injustice or suffering will be totally exterminated is unrealistic. The plan of action helps to root the vision in a contextual reality. I suggest developing no more than five goals in the plan of action. A plan of action that goes beyond this may be too broad for a youth ministry to accomplish. I would rather see a simple plan of action with one goal that was successfully achieved than an elaborate plan of action with five goals and only a few haphazard achievements. Once the plan has been written, it should be put into action.

Movement five: evaluation. The final movement is never final. The reflection-action process is neverending. This movement not only evaluates the plan of action, but continues education and reflection toward future action. In movement five, I suggest five primary questions: What victories can we celebrate from this process? What lessons did we learn from this process—individually and as a group? How successful were we in reaching the goals of our plan of action? How can we better prepare in the future? What injustice or suffering should we address next?

Allow time for an honest, fruitful and introspective sharing. Divide the teens into smaller groups, then gather as a larger group for discussion. Most important, this should be a time of celebration. Whenever youth work toward community transformation, it is time for celebration.

A reflection-action praxis, student copy: Social issue.

Movement one: experience.

- What injustices and suffering are youth experiencing in this community?

Movement two: examination.

- What is the root cause of this injustice or suffering?
- Who are the people and structures in power that benefit from those who are suffering?
- Who are the specific people who are suffering?

Movement three: reflection.

- What do we hope and envision will happen in regard to this issue?
- What is our youth ministry committed to doing?

Movement four: action.

- What is our plan of action to address this issue?

Movement five: evaluation.

- What victories can we celebrate from this process?
- What lessons did we learn from this process—individually and as a group?

- How successful were we in reaching the goals of our plan of action?

- How can we better prepare in the future?

- What injustice or suffering should we address next?

Example two: Communion

Movement one: experience. Initiate the reflection-action praxis by asking two questions: What does Communion mean to you? What does Communion mean in your life? After a few minutes of processing the responses, move on to movement two.

Movement two: examination. The lesson is divided into three parts. First, the class examines the Lord's Supper in Matthew 26:17-30. Offer a brief explanation of the institution of Communion by Jesus. In part two, compare this passage with the passage regarding the fellowship of believers found in Acts 2:42-47. Highlight the fellowship and service aspects associated with Communion. Finally, present the specific teachings of Communion within the congregation's denominational or tradition heritage. If this seems like too much information, simply select the Scripture reading from Matthew.

Movement three: reflection. Following the lesson, ask, What one thing did you find interesting in the lesson? How is the Bible's teaching of Communion the same as or different from your own experience of Communion? How does the description of the fellowship of believers found in Acts influence your understanding of Communion? After two or three minutes of quiet reflection, the students return to the small groups to share their thoughts. Allow time for processing. Remember, this is not a time for debate but a time for sharing and listening.

Movement four: action. The youth group begins to consider how to specifically apply these teachings into their lives. If the action is for individual application, suggest to the students that they identify one way to be better in communion with another person. After several minutes of small-group sharing, the youth worker asks the students to name one specific action each will take this week that will bring him or her more closely into communion with another person. Some of the youth may need clarification. As with all the movements, patiently guide students to a better understanding, helping them to move toward application of a specific action into their lives.

If the action is for communal application, say, "Identify how we, as a youth ministry community, can make the celebration of Communion more meaningful." Again, allow time for private reflection, then small-group processing. Each small group makes a list of ways the youth ministry can make the celebration of Communion more meaningful. Then, each small group makes a presentation to the entire larger youth group. Along with the team, develop a worship service with Communion specifically geared to youth that implements several of the shared responses.

Movement five: evaluation. If the evaluation is for individual application, during the following week, help teens to self-evaluate by saying, "Last week, each person was to perform a specific action which would bring you closer into communion with another person. Let's take a few moments in our small groups to share these experiences."

If the evaluation is for communal application say, "Recently, we discussed how we, as a youth ministry community, can make the celebration of Communion more meaningful. Since then we celebrated a Communion service using several of the shared responses. Let's take a few moments in our small groups to share this experience."

As you can see, I am a strong proponent of small groups. In my experience, most youth will share in a small-group context. However, few will share in a large group. I suggest allowing time for small-group sharing then selecting a spokesperson from each group to share with the larger group. Also invite each small group, one at a time, and require each member to share at least one perspective.

End the evaluation with a closure question, such as, Name one new thing you learned about Communion. What does Communion mean to you now? These nonthreatening questions and statements allow the reflection-action process to end in a positive, reflective and educational way.

A reflection-action praxis, student copy: Communion

Movement one: experience.

- What does Communion mean to you?
- What does Communion mean in your life?

Movement two: examination.

- Read Matthew 26:17-30 (The Lord's Supper)
- Read Acts 2:42-47 (The Fellowship of Believers)

Movement three: reflection.

- What one thing did you find interesting in the lesson?
- How is the Bible's vision of Communion the same as or different from your own experience of Communion?
- How does the description of the fellowship of believers found in Acts affect your understanding of Communion?

Movement four: action.

- Identify one way in which you can better be in communion with another person?
- Individual application: Name one specific action you will take this week that will bring you closer into spiritual communion with another person.
- Communal application: Identify how we, as a youth ministry community, can make the celebration of Communion more meaningful.

Movement five: evaluation.

- Name one new thing you learned about Communion.
- What does Communion mean to you now?

5

Urban Perspective Shifts

FROM THE GARDEN OF EDEN TO THE CITY OF GOD

While prophetic youth ministries are certainly engaged in evangelism and proclaiming the gospel message, this perspective is less about mission fields and more about contextualization. The concept of mission fields seems to have an offensive approach or takeover implication. At its most extreme, it connotes a theological colonialism. Many Christians come into the urban context with a mission-field takeover mentality. Urban ministers find this offensive and presumptuous, for it degrades the dignity of those presently living in the inner city. What makes this even worse is that many churches in the urban context also have this mission-field mentality.

In analyzing various urban models, Eldin Villafañe in *Transforming the City* writes, "Contextualization is the *sine qua non* of all faithful and effective urban theological education. All our examples see the city as a unique context demanding a distinctive response."[1]

Villafañe then quotes Michael Mota:

When does an institution that sees itself as taking its resources "into" the city become part of the urban context? There are real differences in providing education "to, in and with." This raises a significant issue in regard to the meaning and process of contextualization.[2]

---

[1]Eldin Villafañe, Douglas Hall, Efrain Agosto and Bruce W. Jackson, *Seek the Peace of the City: Reflections on Urban Ministry* (Grand Rapids: Eerdmans, 1995), p. 192.
[2]Ibid., p. 193.

The mission field paradigm can never fully be an authentic incarnational presence because missionaries who come *into* the inner city and minister *to* urban people tend to leave the urban context. It is only through a contextualization theology—living *with* and ministering *among* urban people—that an authentic incarnational presence can be realized in the long run.

Orlando Costas offers a powerful image highlighting this shift in contextual missiology as he unpacks Hebrews 13:12, "And so Jesus also suffered outside the city gate to make the people holy through his own blood." Costas explains about Jesus and contextualization,

> He is described in our text as the man of God who dies outside the gate of the Holy City. . . . The death of Jesus outside the gate implies a new place of salvation. In the Old Testament the temple, which had replaced the ancient tabernacle, was understood not just as a place of worship, but especially as the central location of salvation. . . . In this context salvation was confined to the temple, inside the walls of the Holy City. . . . With Jesus there came a fundamental shift in the location of salvation: the center was moved to the periphery. Jesus dies in the wilderness among the outcast and disenfranchised. The unclean and defiled territory became holy ground as he took upon himself the function of the temple. . . . With the change of location came also a shift in focus. The concept of salvation was now seen in a broader and more radical perspective. No longer was it understood in terms of a mere benefit. The focus was now on commitment to a life of service.[3]

The concept of urban contextualization understands evangelism not as a ministry of the church to urban people, but as the incarnation of the church living out the gospel within the urban context.[4]

URBAN CHRIST—FROM JESUS OR CHRIST ALONE TO JESUS CHRIST INCARNATE

In A.D. 451, at the Council of Chalcedon, the gathering of bishops of the universal church declared once and for all that Jesus was fully God and fully man, one person with two natures—divine and human.

---

[3]Orlando Costas, *Christ Outside the Gate* (Maryknoll, N.Y.: Orbis, 1984), pp. 188-89.
[4]This reflection is in no way, shape or form a rejection or condemnation of short mission trips or of Christians who are called to minister in the urban context. Yet, it is a caution for Christians to come with a vision which honors and respects people living in the urban context.

We, then, following the holy Fathers, all with one consent, teach men to confess one and the same Son, our Lord Jesus Christ, perfect in Godhead and also perfect in manhood; very God and very man, of a rational soul and body; coessential with the Father according to the Godhead, and consubstantial with us according to the Manhood; in all things like unto us, without sin; begotten before all ages of the Father according to the Godhead, and in these latter days, for us and for our salvation, born of the Virgin Mary, the God-bearer, according to the Manhood; one and the same Christ, Son, Lord, Only-begotten, to be acknowledged in two natures without confusion, without change, without division, and without separation; the distinction of natures being by no means taken away by the union, but rather the property of each nature being preserved, and concurring in one Person and one Subsistence, not parted or divided into two persons, but one and the same Son, and only begotten, God the Word, the Lord Jesus Christ, as the prophets from the beginning have spoken of him, and the Lord Jesus Christ himself has taught us, and the Creed of the holy Fathers has handed down to us.[5]

I want to stress here that prophetic urban youth workers must have an integrated understanding of the incarnation, both christologically and ministerially. The youth worker must avoid the tendency to overemphasize the human nature (i.e., liberal and activist Jesus) or the divine nature (i.e., traditional Christ) of the incarnated Jesus Christ at the expense of the other. Divorcing the two aspects of the incarnation may potentially lead to relativism, utilitarianism or humanism on the one hand and legalism or moralism on the other hand.

Understanding Christ incarnate also has ministerial implications. The incarnational youth ministry reflects the divine nature of the body of Christ, different from a secular youth program or youth group. This highlights the danger of youth ministries that try to become so relevant to youth that they minimize or compromise the faith component. Youth ministries need not compete with or mimic youth culture. Christian youth ministries have something that no other youth program or youth-culture entity has—a safe and loving place where lives can be transformed in Jesus Christ.

Naturally, this does not mean that youth ministries should not engage

---

[5] See Philip Schaff, *Creeds of Christendom* (Grand Rapids: Baker Academic, 1990), 2:62-63.

youth culture. If they do not, they quickly become irrelevant. However, the incarnation challenges us to be faithful to both the human and the divine nature of the ministry to urban youth. The Jesus-alone youth ministry wants to either *help* youth (i.e., liberal) or *empower* youth (i.e., activist). The Christ-alone youth ministry wants to *save* youth (i.e., traditionalist). The *Christ incarnated* youth ministry wants to *live with and among* youth (i.e., prophetic).

Costas offers three missiological implications of the incarnation which are relevant to prophetic youth ministry in the urban context:

> The first missiological implication of the Incarnation is that of a new and fresh experience of Jesus Christ from within the harsh reality of the hurt, destitute and marginated of the earth. This proceeds from the fact that, in Jesus Christ, God became related with humanity in a radically new way. This meant that the Son of God humbled himself to the extent that he took the form of a servant and thus the identity of the poor, powerless and oppressed.
>
> Another missiological implication of the Incarnation is the historical evaluation of our experiences. . . . The criterion of the life, ministry and death of Jesus Christ permits us to identify him today. The criterion lead us not only to discover who he is (the Lord and Savior of the oppressed), but where he is to be found today (among the poor, the powerless and the oppressed), and what he is doing (healing their wounds, breaking their chains of oppression, demanding justice and peace, giving life and imparting hope).
>
> This brings us to a third missiological implication of the Incarnation for the contextualization of the gospel in the world of the oppressed. Not only must our experience of Christ from below be tested against past historical criterion, . . . but it must also be verified in the transformation of the present situation of the oppressed. . . . He did not suffer and die to leave things as they were but, rather, to bring a new order of life.[6]

Urban youth cannot place their faith in a Christ-alone figure who is so divine that he did not experience or understand the realities of human suffering. Urban youth also cannot place their faith in a Jesus-alone figure who, like so many pseudo-urban messiahs, casts visions of grandeur and ends up either as a false prophet or a social martyr.

---

[6]Costas, *Christ Outside the Gate*, pp. 13-16.

Inner-city urban youth often live in a state of violence, poverty, drugs, discrimination and undereducation. They can identify with an incarnated Jesus Christ with a broken family history, who lived, suffered and died under Roman occupation, then conquered death to rise again. In this Jesus Christ, there is both solidarity and hope.

Incarnational prophetic youth ministry is imbued with this passionate theology. Urban youth—like all youth—are seeking a passionate truth to grasp. Neither the Jesus-alone nor Christ-alone perspective will satisfy.

In the introduction of *Practicing Passion,* Kenda Creasy Dean sets the groundwork for the rest of her book by referring to Eric Erickson's well-known *Identity, Youth and Crisis.* "Adolescents," she writes, "are searching for something, for someone, 'to die for,' to use Eric Erickson's haunting phrase: a cause worthy of their suffering, a love worthy of a lifetime and not just Sunday night."[7] She then begins to weave into this the theological concept of the passion of Christ—the life, death and resurrection of the Son of God. Jesus loves adolescents so passionately that he is willing to die for them. The reciprocal cost is that his love, in turn, requires them to die for him.

Dean eloquently writes,

> Listen closely. Behind these youthful ultimatums is a plea: Please, please tell me it's true. True love is always worth dying for. Please tell me I'm worth dying for. . . . Please show me a God who loves me this much—and who is worth loving passionately in return. Because if Jesus isn't worth dying for, then he's not worth living for, either.[8]

Only an incarnational, theological and ministerial understanding of Jesus Christ will satisfy urban youth. And, ultimately, only a passionate Christ incarnate best exemplifies an urban Christ. Jesus Christ, a member of a minority group, born in a humble setting, to an unwed teenage mother, lives with a stepfather, comes from an imperfect family lineage, lives in a state of Roman occupation near urban centers, travels to other cities throughout Galilee; he argues and condemns the religious and polit-

---

[7]Kenda Creasy Dean, *Practicing Passion: Youth and the Quest for a Passionate Church* (Grand Rapids: Eerdmans, 2004), p. 2.
[8]Ibid., pp. 31-32.

ical leaders of his time, yet is compassionate to sinners and the marginalized; an innocent man, he is given a mock and illegal trial, executed by power structures of his day; yet, in the end, he conquers death, offers words of hope to his believers, sends a helper to be with us and anxiously awaits our reunion again.

URBAN SOTERIOLOGY—FROM PERSONAL SALVATION TO HOLISTIC LIBERATION

All people are in need of salvation. Prophetic spirituality recognizes salvation as both an eschatological and an existential reality. With the birth, life, death and resurrection of Jesus Christ, the in-breaking of the kingdom of God has begun. Therefore, our liberation is not just personal/spiritual, toward a future heaven. It also represents liberation from all things that oppress us and hold us in bondage. Costas explains,

> By the saving grace of Jesus Christ we acquire the gift of obedience to the Lord of History; we are enabled to submit ourselves to the Word of God and to be directed by the Holy Spirit. . . . Obedience to the kingdom of God is, then, the fruit of the grace revealed in Jesus Christ. It is not a precondition to the experience of salvation, but part and parcel of that salvation. Thus, it is not only one of its visible fruits, but also its historical confirmation. . . . In other words, the salvation that is manifest in the gift of obedience is confirmed by obedient action.[9]

Salvation is a concept that is inherent in the biblically orthodox worldview. Salvation represents the liberation from the bondage of sin. And, while it presupposes a transformation in the life of the new believer, it does not necessarily directly address social and systemic sin. Liberation subsumes personal/spiritual salvation with social and systemic bondage. Theologically and philosophically, moving from a salvation worldview to a liberation worldview tends to be more holistic and eliminates the sacred-secular dichotomy.

In the urban context, there is much social/economic bondage from which people need liberation—poverty, unemployment, substance abuse, violence, etc. This is important because Christian evangelism—within the context of the in-breaking of the kingdom of God—is a theology which

---

[9]Costas, *Christ Outside the Gate*, pp. 28-29.

requires present social existential engagement in addition to spiritual eschatological envisioning.

> And he stood up to read. The scroll of the prophet Isaiah was handed to him. Unrolling it, he found the place where it is written:
>
> "The Spirit of the Lord is on me,
>> because he has anointed me
>> to preach good news to the poor.
> He has sent me to proclaim freedom for the prisoners
>> and recovery of sight for the blind,
> to release the oppressed,
>> to proclaim the year of the Lord's favor."
>
> Then he rolled up the scroll, gave it back to the attendant and sat down. The eyes of everyone in the synagogue were fastened on him, and he began by saying to them, "Today this scripture is fulfilled in your hearing." (Luke 4:16-21)

This Scripture passage reflects the inaugural address of Jesus' messianic mission. While this involves personal/spiritual liberation, it also includes

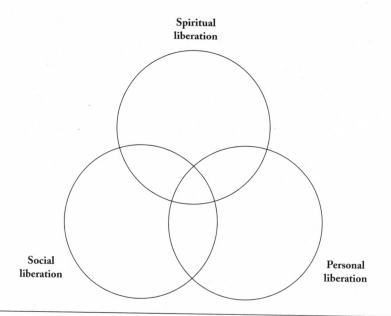

Figure 5.1. Prophetic urban soteriology

social liberation. In *A Theology for Liberation*, Gustavo Gutiérrez writes,

> Sin is not only an impediment to salvation in the afterlife. Insofar as it con-
> stitutes a break with God, sin is a historical reality, it is a breach of the com-
> munion of persons with each other, it is a turning in of individuals on
> themselves which manifests itself in a multifaceted withdrawal from others.
> And because sin is a person and social intra-historical reality, a part of the
> daily events of human life, it is also, and above all, an obstacle to life's reach-
> ing the fullness we call salvation.[10]

URBAN HAMARTIOLOGY—FROM PERSONAL/SPIRITUAL SIN TO SYSTEMIC/ STRUCTURAL SIN

Biblically orthodox Christians have traditionally done a good job of sharing the gospel of redemption. They have generally not developed such a
good history of addressing the social gospel. Listen to the words taken
from the statement of faith of the Urban Family Empowerment Center, a
faith-based initiative whose mission is to holistically empower urban families. These words express the essence of the power of Jesus in response to
social and systemic sin.

> We believe people are created in the image and likeness of God and recog-
> nize the sacred dignity of human life at every stage. While people are capa-
> ble of great good, we are marred by an attitude of personal disobedience
> toward God called sin.
>
> Furthermore, beyond personal sin there also exist social, economic, and
> political sins that create systemic injustice which oppresses people and de-
> means human dignity.
>
> Any injustice or disrespect for human life is an affront to God. Therefore,
> all of creation is in need of liberation, reconciliation, and redemption that
> can only be found through the life, death, and resurrection of Jesus Christ.
>
> While all people are in need of God's love and healing, we are uniquely
> concerned about the urban family, particularly the poor, and stand in soli-
> darity with them. Therefore, we humbly yet boldly accept the call to be a
> lighthouse, spiritually and socially, in the urban community, sharing the
> Good News of Jesus Christ, engaged in personal, spiritual, and social trans-

---

[10]Gustavo Gutiérrez, *A Theology of Liberation*, trans. and ed. Caridad Inda and John Eagleson, with
new introduction (Maryknoll, N.Y.: Orbis, 1988), p. 85.

formation, and committed to the struggle of justice.[11]

The prophetic youth ministry recognizes that social sin is an injustice against God and God's people. In *To Live in Peace*, Mark Gornik addresses this injustice:

> Because human persons are created in God's image, God is harmed when-
> ever any of them are denied standing, sustenance and dignity. Thus the
> wounding of the poor and vulnerable through oppression is not merely
> wrong but . . . an assault on God. On this basis, God and the inner city have
> a claim on the city and other human beings, a claim for right relationships.[12]

This concept of social sin is also self-convicting, for we all must ask our-selves, How have I contributed to communal injustice? In *Seek the Peace of the City*, Eldin Villafañe explains:

> The predicament of *all* persons is death—separation from God, from oth-
> ers, from themselves, and even from creation. Scripture is quite clear that in-
> dividual action has marked social implications. It likewise notes that social
> and corporate action has marked individual implications. Sin, while being
> deeply personal, is not just individualistic.[13]

Do urban youth sin? Of course. But so do corporate conglomerates, the government, the public school system and many other entities. Do urban youth need redemption from sin? Of course. But so do corporate conglom-erates, the government, the public school system and others. Again, Cos-tas offers powerful insight:

> Disobedience, injustice and unbelief are not generic concepts; they are per-
> sonal actions. The Bible teaches that sin is a reality in the life of every human
> being. . . . To say that sin is personal, however, is not to say that its conse-
> quences are limited to the individual. In biblical faith, that which is personal
> is never individualistic, isolated from others. On the contrary, that which is
> personal is intrinsically related to that which is collective. . . . Personal sin

---

[11]The Urban Family Empowerment Center, founded by this writer, was conceived in response to the increasing needs of lower-income inner-city families. Birthed in the South Bronx, it is a private, not-for-profit, faith-based organization whose mission is to holistically empower urban families; see <www.empowerthefamily.org>.

[12]Mark R. Gornik, *To Live in Peace: Biblical Faith and the Changing Inner City* (Grand Rapids: Eerdmans, 2002), p. 52.

[13]Villafañe et al., *Seek the Peace of the City*, p. 16.

brings with it collective guilt. . . . The opposite is equally true, however. Sin is structural as well as personal. It is structural in the sense that it answers to the "logic" behind collective behavior. . . . The totality of these relationships makes up the personality of society. . . . This is why in the Bible there are examples of both personal sins and corporate sins. . . . Institutions disobey God, act unjustly, and set themselves up as gods. . . . Because sin is a universal problem, its eradication must be radical. It is impossible to speak of a purely personal salvation, because that would leave social sin intact. Nor is it possible to speak exclusively of social salvation, because that would leave untouched the personal root of sin. Salvation, to be truly effective, must be salvation of the soul and of the body, of the individual and society, of humanity and of the whole creation groaning in travail together.[14]

URBAN SPIRITUALITY—FROM PERSONAL SPIRITUALITY TO HOLISTIC SPIRITUALITY

Biblically orthodox Christians have long been guilty of dualism: separating the spiritual from the social and physical realm. Prophetic youth ministry in the urban context moves to a more holistic spirituality. This includes addressing and integrating the personal, spiritual and social dimension. Villafañe explains:

> If the whole church is to take the whole Gospel to the whole world, it must have a "wholistic" spirituality. A spirituality, if it is to be authentic and relevant, should correlate with all of life; for after all the Spirit of the Lord, who leads and empowers, must lead and empower all areas of our life. . . . Thus the double focus and goal of Christian spirituality has 1) a vertical focus—the continual transformation into the likeness of Jesus, the resurrected Lord and 2) a horizontal focus—the following of Jesus, in similar obedience of the Father's missional calling.[15]

Prophetic urban spirituality is vulnerable and honest. It is also political, for it engages in the systems and structures affecting the lives of youth. In *A Lesson of Urban Spirituality*, Valerie Russell writes in hard-hitting fashion,

> Urban spirituality is more than vague platitudes about caring about one another in the "God loves you; so do I" mode. It means, rather, radical engagement with the stranger, resembling more, the attitude of "God loves you; and

---

[14]Costas, *Christ Outside the Gate*, p. 26.
[15]Villafañe et al., *Seek the Peace of the City*, pp. 12-13.

I'm trying." A strong spirituality for the city requires a theological belief system that stems from hard-hitting critical social analysis, a process that seeks harmony between the discipline of meditation and commitment to an action based agenda—the mind and heart seeking to "know" God and act accordingly.[16]

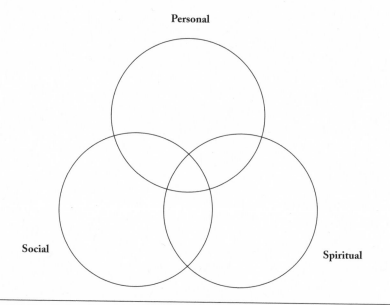

Figure 5.2. Prophetic urban spirituality

URBAN SOLIDARITY—FROM UPWARD MOBILITY TO DOWNWARD MOBILITY

Urban youth ministry is primarily ministry to poor youth. Prophetic urban youth ministers have a "preferential option for the poor." This phrase reflects a deep compassion for the poor and vulnerable. "The 'poor' includes but is not limited to those who are economically deprived. The principle is rooted in the biblical notion of justice, where God calls us to be advocates for the voiceless and powerless among us . . . and where right relationships are restored. Regardless of the reasons, those who are in any way deprived or who are particularly vulnerable have a special moral claim on the community."[17]

[16]Valerie E. Russell, "A Lesson on Urban Spirituality," in *Envisioning the New City: A Reader on Urban Ministry,* ed. Eleanor Scott Meyers (Louisville: Westminster John Knox, 1992), p. 190.
[17]This description is taken from "Preferential Option for the Poor," Ascension Healthcare <www.ascensionhealth.org/ethics/public/issues/preferential.asp>.

Let us say a parent has two children. One child is healthy and the other is chronically sick. Which child does the parent love more? Of course, the parent loves both children equally. However, the child who is sick requires more assistance, attention and time. The parent is cautious not to neglect the healthy child, but this is the reality of caring for a child in need. It is the same with urban youth ministry. Those who are poor need more of our assistance, attention and time. They are particularly vulnerable.

The following story in Matthew rings very true for the prophetic urban youth worker:

> While Jesus was having dinner at Matthew's house, many tax collectors and "sinners" came and ate with him and his disciples. When the Pharisees saw this, they asked his disciples, "Why does your teacher eat with tax collectors and 'sinners'?"
>
> On hearing this, Jesus said, "It is not the healthy who need a doctor, but the sick. But go and learn what this means: 'I desire mercy, not sacrifice.' For I have not come to call the righteous, but sinners." (Matthew 9:10-13)

Prophetic youth ministry incorporates Leonardo and Clodovis Boff's five theological reasons for the option for the poor, as written in *Introducing Liberation Theology*. First, there is theological motivation (on God's part). As Creator and Father, God feels compelled to come to the aid of the oppressed poor, his suffering children (Exodus 3:7-9). Second, there is christological motivation (on Christ's part). Christ undeniably made a personal option for the poor and held them to be the main recipients of his message (Luke 6:20; 7:21-22). Third, there is eschatological motivation (from the standpoint of the final judgment). The gospel points out that at the final judgment, when our eternal salvation or damnation will be decided, what will count will be our attitude toward and acceptance or rejection of the poor (Matthew 25:31-46). Fourth, there is apostolic motivation (on the part of the apostles). The apostles and their followers held all things in common so that there would be no poor among them (Acts 2:42-47; 4:32-37). Finally, there is ecclesiological motivation (on the part of the church). Because of the immense suffering in the world, prophetic youth ministry seeks to urge all Christians to live their faith in a way that transforms society in the direction toward greater justice. "All need to make the option for the poor: the rich with generosity and no regard for reward, the poor for their fellow poor and those who are even poorer than they."[18]

Jesus always displayed a preferential option for those who are most vulnerable, such as the lepers, women, sinners and children. He desires mercy and compassion. Prophetic urban youth workers are comfortable with tax collectors, sinners and the sick.

URBAN JUSTICE—FROM CONCERN TO COMPASSION

When urban teens say, "I feel you," this suggests something very serious. It is more than simply an intellectual understanding of what someone is saying. This speaks of *pathos:* "I feel your pain, your joy, your anger."

Leonard and Clodovis Boff explain how compassion is the heart of liberation theology:

> Without a minimum of "suffering with" this suffering that affects the great majority of the human race, liberation theology can neither exist nor be understood. Underlying liberation theology is a prophetic and comradely commitment to the life, cause, and struggle of these millions of debased and marginalized human beings, a commitment to ending this historical-social inequality.[19]

Christ personifies the compassion of God. Throughout the Gospels, we read the stories of Jesus' compassion for others, a deep and primal love for them. This compassion moves beyond concern for justice.

Social justice is different from social reform, social analysis and social service. Social reform seeks to improve the situation of the suffering but remains within the existing social relationships and the basic structures of society. Social analysis asks the structural and systemic questions (pedagogy). This involves reflection. Therefore, social analysis views social reform as insufficient. Social service distributes products and services (practice/charity). This involves action. Ultimately, it is social justice which engages both analysis and action to move beyond reform toward transformation by way of praxis.

---

[18]Leonardo Boff and Clodovis Boff, *Introducing Liberation Theology* (Maryknoll, N.Y.: Orbis, 1987), pp. 44-46.
[19]Ibid., p. 3.

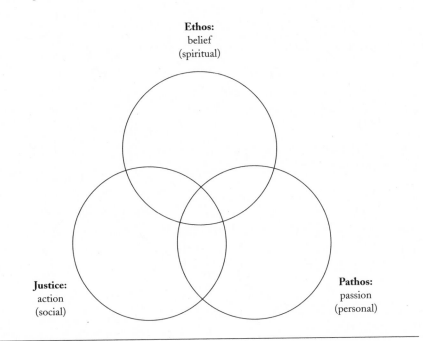

Ethos:
belief
(spiritual)

Justice:
action
(social)

Pathos:
passion
(personal)

Figure 5.3. Prophetic urban justice

URBAN KOINONIA—FROM THEM TO US

The shift from *them* to *us* naturally flows from the previous movement of mission fields to contextualization. When one has a *mission fields* worldview, the ministry structure is designed for *them*. When one has a *contextualization* worldview, the ministry structure is designed for *us*.

It is not uncommon for people in the church to refer to "those kids." Prophetic youth workers see all youth as *ours*. This is particularly challenging to youth workers who view only those who attend the youth ministry as ours. This is one reason so many teens do not attend church—they are made to feel like outsiders.

With regard to koinonia, Villafañe writes, "It speaks to us of solidarity and community. In biblical Christianity koinonia is a mark of maturity—of true spirituality."[20] Urban koinonia demonstrates authentic partnership and collaboration with those in the urban context.

---

[20]Villafañe, *Transforming the City*, p. 198.

URBAN LOVE—FROM PSEUDO-HOSPITALITY TO AUTHENTIC HOSPITALITY

Prophetic youth ministry is hospitable to all youth and their families, regardless of their status and reputation. While this may seem obvious, I have witnessed churches embrace only those youth and families who act a certain way. These "accepted youth" may be expected to dress, speak and behave a certain way. In many churches in the city, "problem youth" are simply not always welcome. Many teens in our community are not living the ideals of the Christian faith. Yet, prophetic youth ministries engage in radical hospitality, welcoming all youth in all their messiness.

I am always profoundly struck when I examine Jesus' family lineage. (See Matthew 1:1-6 and Luke 3:23-38.) At the top of his family tree is Adam, who initiated original sin; Jacob, who, along with his mother (Rebekah), deceived his father (Isaac) and brother (Esau) for the birthright; Tamar, a Canaanite, who birthed a child (Perez) out of wedlock; Rahab, a Canaanite, who ran a brothel and lied on behalf of Joshua's spies; Ruth, a Moabite, from the lineage of Sodom, who married Boaz, an Israelite; David, who had one of his most faithful soldiers (Uriah) killed in order to marry the man's wife (Bathsheba); Bathsheba, who became pregnant through an adulterous affair with David while she was married; Solomon, who later in life became filled with pride at his accomplishments, had over 700 wives and 300 concubines, and built many shrines to the pagan gods of the women he married; and, of course, Jesus' mother, Mary, an out-of-wedlock pregnant teenage girl.

This "messiness" is not an uncommon family scenario in the urban context. In *A Theology as Big as the City*, Ray Bakke offers this interesting insight into Jesus' family:

> Jesus was the product of an international family tree. . . . On the divine side, Jesus was the virgin-born son of God. Let there be no doubt about that. . . . But on the human side . . . Jesus was also very human indeed. He choreographed into his own earthly body all the most theologically sinful bloodlines in the Middle East. In a very real sense, this opening paragraph smashes racism. Jesus was the mixed-racial Savior of the world.[21]

What is important here with regard to prophetic youth ministry is the

---

[21]Ray Bakke, *A Theology as Big as the City* (Downers Grove, Ill.: InterVarsity Press, 1997), p. 125.

intentionality of welcoming all teens by breaking down the barriers that exist between the local church/youth ministry and neighborhood youth. Gornik beautifully explains the church's role of biblical imperative of hospitality within the urban context:

When "welcome" is set within a theological framework of God's grace in Christ, important implications emerge for the church in the area of family life, neighborhood youth and the development of worship space. First, a community of welcome embraces all families. Family life is under intense social, economic, and cultural pressure in the inner city. How is the church to welcome families under such pressure? The church's call to support families is first a call to care for them in whatever form they take. We do well to remember that there are few—if any—examples of "ideal" families in Scripture! The church is to be a community where all families are welcomed, loved, and supported. Is this not something of the meaning of the biblical injunction to take special care of the widow and the orphan? Instead of focusing on the negatives, it is better to begin by looking at the strengths of inner-city families, fathers and mothers, building them up from the perspective of their strengths. . . .

Our inner cities are filled with many Latino and African-American youth searching in the wrong places and the wrong ways for identity and meaning. Alienated from mainstream avenues of opportunities and education, they are at risk for joining a gang, using drugs and dropping out of school. But in order to reach them effectively, the church must understand them. . . . The church will often need to seek forgiveness for the way in which it has excluded young people in the past, and to consider possibilities for new directions. . . .

Youth ministry should be given new priority and focus. . . .

Ideally, a church and its building embrace the city, recognizing that all of the city belongs to God. In fact, as a central site of God's passionate concern and presence, the inner city is "holy ground." When ecclesial space is "superior" people of little means often feel it is inappropriate for them to come into such a place. The best "church building" may not be one set apart for worship, but one designed or adapted for community ministry. . . . A church building should make families feel comfortable as they enter it and teenagers look forward to "hanging out" in it. A "come as you are" policy for dress supports this friendly feeling. And whether the church is a traditional tall-steepled building or a store front, it should express beauty in some way; that will also draw people in. Every inner-city church, if it makes the effort, can communicate that it exists to be part of its neighborhood, not beyond or above it. Inner-city neighborhoods need fresh visions of the church as a welcoming community.[22]

URBAN LEADERSHIP—FROM RELOCATING LEADERSHIP TO INDIGENOUS LEADERSHIP

Unquestionably, God can and does use people from outside of the city to minister to and transform an urban neighborhood. I have heard these stories and know personally youth workers who have transitioned into the city and are engaged in successful ministry. However, although dramatic and inspiring, these stories are few and far between. The fact remains that the overwhelming majority of inner-city churches and youth ministries, at least in New York, tend to be led by people from the inner city. It is my contention that the most effective and influential ministries are formed when we shift from relocation leadership to indigenous leadership. Listen to these instructions to the Israelites:

> When you enter the land the LORD your God is giving you and have taken possession of it and settled in it, and you say, "Let us set a king over us like all the nations around us," be sure to appoint over you the king the LORD your God chooses. He must be from among your own brothers. Do not place a foreigner over you, one who is not a brother Israelite. (Deuteronomy 17:14-15)

Prophetic youth ministry must be committed to raising leaders from within the ministry. It is important to note that prophetic urban youth leaders do not always reflect what is considered an idealistic model. Many urban leaders are single moms, divorced dads, grandparents, ex-gang members or high school dropouts. Yet, as Christians, we should believe that God can transform anyone into a leader. The Bible is filled with such characters.

Some have used the phrase "reproductive leadership," meaning the ability to raise up and reproduce leaders from within the community. However, I have also seen "relocated" leaders who have reproduced leaders into a model that is not indigenous to the community. Furthermore, I have also

---

[22]Gornik, *To Live in Peace*, pp. 80-83.

seen relocated leadership teams reproduce effective leaders, but those emerging leaders do not seem to be raised to the upper echelon in terms of decision-making authority.

On the other hand, there are many churches run by people who should not be in positions of leadership. I will be the first to admit that many of our current leaders in the inner city need more development. However, for urban community transformation to occur, ultimately the leadership must be prophetic indigenous leadership.

URBAN THEOLOGY—FROM *SCHOLASTICUS ACADEMICUS* TO *LOCUS THEOLOGICUS*

For prophetic youth ministry to be effective, it must understand and wrestle with theology engaged in the real-life struggles of young people within their context, *locus theologicus*. Accomplishing this requires a transition from *scholasticus academicus*, theology as expressed in the academy or seminary.

If theology is not in dialogue with or engaged in the locus of the people, it remains an abstract theory. A seminary professor once warned, "As you go up the academic ladder, be careful not to forget the language of the people."

In *Seek the Peace of the City*, Villafañe affirms this insight as he both challenges and cautions Latino educators:

> I am deeply concerned that our academic training and often the locus of our academic service disengages us from the *Pueblo*. Scholarship as *Sanadora* requires that we be *presentes* with our Pueblo. Some of us have paid the price in being "too much" of a presence, perhaps to the detriment of quantitative scholarly production. Yet, one hopes that this presence with our Pueblo will result in qualitative scholarly output.[23]

Lynn Rhodes and Nancy Richardson offer another powerful perspective in their essay "Contextualization of Theological Education." They address the shifting of power when theology is done through dialogue in the locus of the community instead of the academy.

> Theology, then, is not a dogma but a dialogical process, an encounter with the contradictions and insights of life itself. . . .

---

[23]Villafañe, *Seek the Peace of the City*, p. 10.

When the larger community is the context, there is a broader dialogical "testing" of legitimate authorities. A seminary-based faculty member who enters into such dialogue may find that her or his particular training and expertise are being challenged because the assumptions of the context are different from those in the seminary. . . . At a basic level, changing the turf changes the dynamics of power; a shift in levels of discomfort takes place. It is no longer just the community-based "teacher" who must enter the academic arena and "adjust" to norms and expectations; it is now the seminary-based faculty and students who enter the community and must learn language and symbols that give meaning to life in that place. . . . As long as theological education is based in the academy, community-based resource people must adjust to the rules of the academy. . . . Changing the locus changes the rules: The community-based person is still teaching in an academic program, but in one with a focus on community, so both academic and community norms and insights apply. No one person or group owns the power to define the rules, and genuine collaboration is possible, even though comfort levels are often disturbed.[24]

With that said, the community also needs the academy. On the one hand, "the fear of the LORD is the beginning of knowledge" (Proverbs 1:7). On the other hand, "the discerning heart seeks knowledge" (Proverbs 15:14). An area of frustration for me comes from biblically orthodox churches in the urban context who minimize or dismiss liberal arts education. We certainly want youth to grow in their faith in Christ, but we must also want them to grow intellectually. How else can we transform urban communities? How else will they penetrate the complicated matrix of life and relationships? The urban church must desire and encourage the intellectual growth of our youth with as much fervency as it devotes to spreading the gospel. Prophetic youth ministries desire to integrate both realities—the development of the faith and the development of the mind. This has never been stressed more poignantly than by Dr. Charles Malik at the opening of the Billy Graham Center at Wheaton College:

If you win the whole world and lose the mind of the world, you will soon

---

[24]Lynn Rhodes and Nancy Richardson, "Contextualization of Theological Education," in *Envisioning the New City: A Reader on Urban Ministry,* ed. Eleanor Scott Meyers (Louisville: Westminster John Knox, 1992), pp. 352, 355.

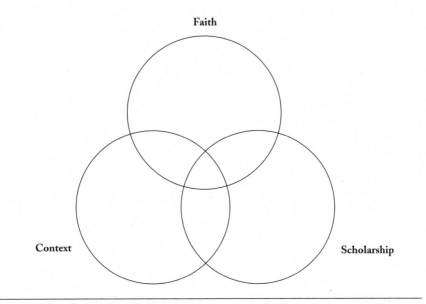

Figure 5.4. Prophetic urban theology

discover you have not won the world. Indeed it may turn out that you have actually lost the world. . . . Responsible Christians face two tasks—that of saving the soul and that of saving the mind.[25]

Prophetic youth ministry engaging in theological and philosophical discourse involves three groups in perpetual conversation: the professor, the youth worker and youth.[26] Professors are the first group, representing the prophetic academic perspective. The blessing of academicians is their gift to analyze, criticize and theorize about the prophetic dimension. Their contributions help youth pastors to re-envision and re-imagine youth ministry.[27]

---

[25]Charles Malik, *The Two Tasks* (Wheaton: Crossway, 1980), pp. 42, 44. See Billy Graham Center Dedication Archives <www.wheaton.edu/bgc/archives/BGCdedication.htm>.

[26]This reflection is adapted from Boff and Boff, *Introducing Liberation Theology*, pp. 11-16.

[27]One example of professors helping youth workers is the Association of Youth Ministry Educators (AYME). AYME is North America's only professional organization for those who teach youth ministry at the undergraduate or graduate level. In addition to holding an annual conference, they also produce the *Journal of Youth Ministry*. The journal offers academic and scholarly essays on the current state of youth ministry, as well as research notes, critical book reviews and other insightful studies. Visit the Association of Youth Ministry Educators' website, <www.aymeducators.org>. Another organization is the International Association for the Study of Youth Ministry. As the name implies, the members' aim is to support and develop the professionalization of youth ministry around the world. They too put out a periodical, *Journal of Youth and Theology*. Visit the International Association for the Study of Youth Ministry website, <www.iasym.org/index.html>.

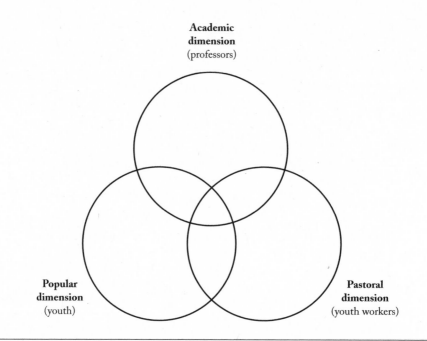

Academic
dimension
(professors)

Popular
dimension
(youth)

Pastoral
dimension
(youth workers)

Figure 5.5. The three groups in the prophetic youth ministry conversation

Prophetic youth workers are the second group in the conversation, representing the prophetic pastoral perspective. Of course, this would include other pastoral leaders, such as lead pastors, priests, elders, deacons, brothers, nuns and other pastoral workers. However, at the heart of prophetic youth ministry engagement is the prophetic youth worker who is doing the day-to-day work with urban teens.

The third and most important group in this conversation consists of the youth themselves. They represent the prophetic popular dimension. While youth are our primary target group, the popular dimension also includes their families and friends.

All three groups should be engaged in conversation. Professors and youth workers should be in dialogue with each other. Youth workers should want to increase their training in order to become more effective in the ministry. They should learn more about adolescent development, age-appropriate education and so on. Also, professors need to hear from youth workers about what's happening in the field. They need to learn what models work and don't work and what's new in the lives of these urban young people. Finally, professors need to be in dialogue with youth. A professor who is not engaged in conversation with youth in some capacity will soon become irrelevant.

URBAN HEAVEN—FROM THE GARDEN OF EDEN TO THE CITY OF GOD

> Then I saw a new heaven and a new earth, for the first heaven and the first earth had passed away, and there was no longer any sea. I saw the Holy City, the new Jerusalem, coming down out of heaven from God, prepared as a bride beautifully dressed for her husband. And I heard a loud voice from the throne saying, "Now the dwelling of God is with men, and he will live with them. They will be his people, and God himself will be with them and be their God. He will wipe every tear from their eyes. There will be no more death or mourning or crying or pain, for the old order of things has passed away."
>
> He who was seated on the throne said, "I am making everything new!"
>
> I did not see a temple in the city, because the Lord God Almighty and the Lamb are its temple. The city does not need the sun or the moon to shine on it, for the glory of God gives it light, and the Lamb is its lamp. The nations will walk by its light, and the kings of the earth will bring their splendor into it. On no day will its gates ever be shut, for there will be no night there. The glory and honor of the nations will be brought into it. Nothing impure will ever enter it, nor will anyone who does what is shameful or deceitful, but only those whose names are written in the Lamb's book of life. (Revelation 21:1-5, 22-27)

One of the most significant gifts a prophetic urban youth ministry can offer is the vision of a transformed city and the hope of a New Jerusalem. When Christians speak of a new city, they are referring to both an existential and an eschatological reality. The image of a place with no more death, mourning, crying or pain is a blessed hope for the urban context.

This is also contrasted with another city—Babylon. Biblically speaking, Babylon has always come to symbolize the city which is anti-God. Bakke explains:

> Babylon was also the destroyer of Jerusalem, its temple and monarchy. . . . In Revelation Babylon is the code name for Rome. . . . The 1 Peter text applies the exile metaphor to the church, for Christians were dispersed throughout Rome as Jews had been in ancient Babylon. . . . Revelation

teaches that history will climax in a battle between two titans, the earthly city of Babylon and the heavenly city of Jerusalem.[28]

For many urban people, the inner city feels like Babylon. But, it is the hope of God's New City—the New Jerusalem—that makes us smile and dance. Prophetic youth ministries must always share this image of hope—of a promised new city—to youth and their families. For many, it is the only hope they have.

---

[28]Bakke, *A Theology as Big as the City*, pp. 184-85.

PART TWO

Interdisciplinary Dimensions

6

Theory, Theology and Praxis

My doctoral mentor often said, "There is nothing more practical than good theory." Unfortunately, many youth ministers jump over theory and go directly to practice. That is, they tend not to spend enough time reflecting on the deeper philosophical and theological issues of ministry to youth and spend too much time on programming issues. There is also the tendency to remain in the theological realm without engaging other theoretical perspectives, particularly the social sciences. James Mohler passionately states,

> The bottom line is that to be effective in ministry, one must have more than knowledge about the liberal arts; one must have an integrated and practical understanding of the liberal arts. Not only do these various disciplines help us relate to the people with whom we are called to minister, but they also help us understand God in all of his infinite wonder and glory. . . . We need to invite cross-disciplinary discussion into our classrooms. We need to point out to students when we are drawing from the various disciplines as they help inform us about ministry, and as they have challenged our own personal perspectives of life. . . .
>
> Not only do those of us in ministry need to think theologically, but we need to understand the social sciences as well. We need to not only understand about sociology, but we need to be able to "exegete" a culture. Because a worker in ministry works with people, psychology is an important discipline, as it helps one to understand the nature of how people think and feel. It is not enough for the worker to know about psychology, but he or she must be able to integrate theology and psychology, seeking to find the best way to promote healing in a person. . . . In addition, the person in ministry should

have an historical perspective, not simply a knowledge of history, but an understanding of history strong enough to be able to highlight God's eternal plan and His faithfulness throughout history. This may help us give perspective to people that are struggling with life, offering hope in dark times.[1]

Pamela Erwin concurs and aptly addresses this matter within the context of youth ministry education when she writes,

> Good theology and good social science are not mutually exclusive activities. . . . In the last fifteen to twenty years, the field of youth ministry education has matured from a primary emphasis on skill-based practitioners to a discipline that is multi-disciplinary in nature, drawing instructors not only from the professional ministry arena, but from the disciplines of anthropology, sociology, psychology as well as theology. . . . Youth ministry graduates must be equipped with an understanding that good youth ministry practice comes from integrative reflection that brings together theology and social science. In this way, students must learn to exegete culture as well as exegeting scripture.[2]

ENGAGING THEORY AND THEOLOGY WITH PRAXIS

The above engagement, while necessary, must also include or lead to action; otherwise it remains a philosophical or theoretical construct. As Erwin asserts, "Youth ministry education should be an integrative discipline that incorporates a three-strand approach of practice, theology and social science. In this approach, one is not pitted against another, but informs and develops the others."[3]

Erwin punctuates these sentiments when she argues,

> Theology is worthless if it does not help us better understand God and his people. Social science is worthless if it does not help us better understand what it means to be human beings created in the image of our Creator God. . . . Effective youth ministry praxis builds from good theology and good social science.[4]

---

[1] James W. Mohler, "Youth Ministry Education and the Liberal Arts: The Need for Integration," *Journal of Youth Ministry* 2, no. 2 (Spring 2004): 58, 57.

[2] Pamela Erwin, "Youth Ministry Education: Where Practice, Theology and Social Science Intersect," *The Journal of Youth Ministry* 4, no. 2 (Spring 2006): 11, 9, 16-17.

[3] Ibid., p. 11.

[4] Ibid.

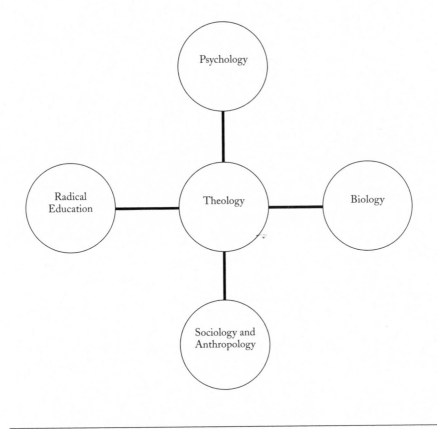

Figure 6.1. Engaging theology with other theoretical perspectives

This chapter discusses the application of theology in youth ministry, but chapters six through ten will explore four theoretical areas that are also crucial to prophetic youth ministry: (1) psychology, (2) biology, (3) sociology and anthropology, and (4) radical education.[5]

THE CHALLENGE OF THEOLOGY TO THE PROPHETIC YOUTH WORKER

While youth workers should become familiar with the other theoretical disciplines, the prophetic youth worker *is* a theologian, a practical theolo-

---

[5]This chapter only briefly examines theology. Its aim is to invite the reader to consider more intentionally the engagement between theology and the other theoretical disciplines. It also provides the template which will be used in the following chapters.

gian.[6] A youth worker draws on the various theoretical subjects, but is not an expert on the subject. A youth worker *is* a theologian because of the act of God and the youth worker's following of the act/ministry of God.[7] Kenda Creasy Dean states the basis for this understanding: "Approaching youth ministry from the perspective of practical theology assumes that youth are called to take part in every practice of Christian ministry, to participate in the total mission of the church, for God calls all of us into the divine plan of salvation."[8]

Prophetic theology, of course, addresses the spiritual issues of youth ministry. The prophetic youth worker, first and foremost, helps urban youth to grow as Christian disciples—deepening and growing in their relationship with Jesus Christ. He or she also recognizes urban youth as disciples called to ministry. Without the theological dimension, the youth ministry becomes a youth program or youth club. The theological foundation of Jesus Christ is what makes a youth program a Christian youth ministry. Dean correctly states,

> Theological reflection keeps the practice of youth ministry focused on God instead of on us. It makes possible radical congruency between what we say we believe and how we conduct our lives. Without intentional theological reflection in our ministries with young people, we will all be living like atheists in no time.[9]

The challenge is to avoid theological extremism, as is the case in the various paradigms. Some youth ministries, such as liberal youth ministries, tend to underemphasize the lordship and messianic significance of Jesus. Others tend to overemphasize legalism or ritualism, such as some tradi-

---

[6]For more information on youth ministry and practical theology, see Kenda Creasy Dean, "Theological Rocks—First Things First," in *Starting Right: Thinking Theologically About Youth Ministry,* ed. Kenda Creasy Dean, Chap Clark and Dave Rahn (Grand Rapids: Zondervan, 2001), pp. 15-26. For more information on practical theology itself, see Ray S. Anderson, *The Shape of Practical Theology: Empowering Ministry with Theological Praxis* (Downers Grove, Ill.: InterVarsity Press, 2001); Friedrich Schweitzer, Johannes A. Van Der Ven and J. A. Van Der Ven, eds., *Practical Theology—International Perspectives* (Frankfurt am Main: Peter Lang, 1999); Paul H. Ballard and John Pritchard, *Practical Theology in Action: Christian Thinking in the Service of the Church and Society* (London: SPCK, 1996); Don S. Browning, *A Fundamental Practical Theology: Descriptive and Strategic Proposals* (Minneapolis: Fortress, 1991); Maureen R. O'Brien, "Practical Theology and Postmodern Religious Education," *Religious Education* 2, no. 2 (1999): 53-63.

[7]I am indebted to the insight provided by an unknown manuscript reader.

[8]Dean, "Theological Rocks," p. 19.

[9]Ibid., p. 29.

tional youth ministries, while still others tend to overemphasize social engagement at the expense of biblical orthodoxy.

As previously mentioned, prophetic youth ministry envisions and develops a ministry which addresses the spiritual, personal and social needs of youth. Theologically speaking, it is built upon three interlocking theological components: (1) a traditional understanding of the Holy Bible and Christian orthodoxy; (2) the spiritual, personal and emotional development of youth; and (3) social justice.

TEENS ARE THEOLOGIANS

Teens are theologians. They reflect on the things of life and wonder where God is, what God thinks, what their response should be. While this reflection may or may not be filtered through a biblical paradigm or through a formal theological process, they are, nonetheless, engaging with questions of ultimate meaning. Dean's insight is helpful in this regard:

Questions to Ponder

Are your youth ministry's theological perspectives too narrow? Is there any space or hospitality for other Christians outside of your personal theological perspective? Does your youth ministry develop healthy Christian disciples? Do you find your youth hospitable to Christians outside of your own specific tradition or denomination? Are your youth growing in the Christian faith? Does your youth ministry teach the incarnation reality of Jesus of Nazareth and Jesus the Christ? Or does it tend to overemphasize one perspective at the expense of the other?

> Most adolescents engage in *intuitive theology*—reflection about the divine-human relationship that often bypasses language and rational discourse, but nonetheless constitutes a real part of a young person's inner life. Intuitive theology might be composed of beliefs that "feel" right to a teenager. . . . If a teenager has been involved in a religious community, she might have an *embedded theology*. Embedded theology comes from a religious story inherited from a faith community. . . . The alternative to intuitive or embedded theology is *deliberate theology*—an understanding of faith that arises when a young person carefully examines his theological assumptions and practices. Deliberate theology is not simply a rational exercise in critical thinking. . . . Deliberate theology is *faith*—it is faith seeking understanding.[10]

---

[10]Ibid., p. 30.

HOW THEOLOGY HELPS THE PROPHETIC YOUTH WORKER

- A biblically rooted and orthodox theology helps the prophetic youth worker to remain Christ centered.
- A healthy theology keeps the prophetic youth worker focused on eschatological truth while struggling with existential realities.
- In a world of ongoing new fads, spiritual ambiguity, cultural and moral relativism, and the various challenges of inner-city living, a Christian theological perspective gives one hope and meaning in life's many struggles and the challenges of youth ministry.

BIBLICAL PERSPECTIVES ON THEOLOGY

The Bible is filled with many references affirming a theological perspective—too many to be addressed. However, there are certain Scripture passages that I wish to highlight for prophetic youth workers in order to inform their theological perspective.

This first passage is a foundational theological emphasis on the need to be born again, recreated, recommitted and refashioned in Christ. Youth should know that they can change if they place their faith in Christ.

> In reply Jesus declared, "I tell you the truth, no one can see the kingdom of God unless he is born again."
>
> "How can a man be born when he is old?" Nicodemus asked. "Surely he cannot enter a second time into his mother's womb to be born!"
>
> Jesus answered, "I tell you the truth, no one can enter the kingdom of God unless he is born of water and the Spirit. Flesh gives birth to flesh, but the Spirit gives birth to spirit." (John 3:3-6)

Teens, like the rest of us, make many mistakes. While it is essential to teach youth to take responsibility for their actions and the boundaries of Christian freedom, it is also vital for them to know their sins will be forgiven if they confess them and are genuinely contrite. One of the most beautiful practices of the Catholic, Orthodox and Episcopal traditions is the sacrament of penance or reconciliation. Under the wisdom of the priest, a person may confess his or her sins and experiences the gift of absolution. While one may debate the specific theology of this practice, it underscores the importance of having a ritual in which people can experience and celebrate the gift of forgiveness. Unfortunately, most Protestant youth ministries do not have a formal ritual of forgiveness. For Bible-believing youth ministries, this is essential. On the one hand, we certainly do not want teens to think that every time they do something wrong they have lost their salvation. On the other hand, when sin is committed, there should be a safe place and ritual, either individually or collectively, that helps them address this issue within a spiritual context and allows them to experience the blessing from the community of faith.[11]

> Then Peter came to Jesus and asked, "Lord, how many times shall I forgive my brother when he sins against me? Up to seven times?"
>
> Jesus answered, "I tell you, not seven times, but seventy-seven times." (Matthew 18:21-22)

The next passage emphasizes the primacy of one's faith over against the things of this temporal life. Marketing in youth culture tends to bombard teens with messages of materialism and accumulation. It is essential to offer youth an alternative perspective in order to help them move from selfishness to otherness: "What good is it for a man to gain the whole world, yet forfeit his soul?" (Mark 8:36).

Yet, the next two passages challenge us not to develop a self-righteous theology.

> If anyone says, "I love God," yet hates his brother, he is a liar. For anyone who does not love his brother, whom he has seen, cannot love God, whom he has not seen. And he has given us this command: Whoever loves God must also love his brother. (1 John 4:20-21)

> And if you do good to those who are good to you, what credit is that to you? Even "sinners" do that. (Luke 6:33)

Finally, the following passage underscores the heart of the Christian faith. It is also a challenge to youth workers, urging them to reach out and minister to youth with whom they do not feel comfortable.

---

[11]Several books which examine spiritual disciplines, discernment and rituals are Mike King, *Presence-Centered Youth Ministry: Guiding Students into Spiritual Formation* (Downers Grove, Ill.: InterVarsity Press, 2006); David F. White, *Practicing Discernment with Youth: A Transformative Youth Ministry Approach* (Cleveland: Pilgrim, 2005); Mark Yaconelli, *Contemplative Youth Ministry: Practicing the Presence of Jesus* (Grand Rapids: Zondervan, 2006).

Hearing that Jesus had silenced the Sadducees, the Pharisees got together. One of them, an expert in the law, tested him with this question: "Teacher, which is the greatest commandment in the Law?"

Jesus replied: "'Love the Lord your God with all your heart and with all your soul and with all your mind.' This is the first and greatest commandment. And the second is like it: 'Love your neighbor as yourself.' All the Law and the Prophets hang on these two commandments." (Matthew 22:34-40)

THE DANGERS OF THEOLOGICAL EXTREMISM

- Theological extremism leads to dogmatism, legalism, ritualism and judgmentalism.

- Theological extremism, at the expense of recognizing social-cultural struggles, may disconnect one from addressing systemic sin or becoming engaged in social action.

- Theological overemphasis on a personal relationship with Jesus Christ may lead to an unhealthy spiritual individualism.

- Theological extremism may lead to overspiritualizing every bad happening. This also leads many youth ministries to address only spiritual issues and to do so through a perspective of theological extremism.

7

The Psychology of Urban Youth

The prophetic youth worker should become familiar with basic adolescent development; prophetic theology addresses these issues. The insights of this field have been a rich blessing for youth ministry. Youth workers can now minister to youth more effectively through a better understanding of how and why adolescents think and behave.

The term *youth* is a sociological construct. Generally speaking, it identifies a certain social group, usually those between childhood and maturity.[1] *Adolescence* refers to a specific stage of development prior to maturity.[2]

This distinction is significant because we tend to interchange these words, which are related but reflect distinct fields of study. Youth workers should familiarize themselves with the various stages of adolescent development. The limitations of this book preclude an exhaustive study of adolescent development. However, what is essential is the awareness that youth workers become familiar with the thinking and behavior of adolescents in order to better understand them and more effectively minister to them.

Generally speaking, developmentalism understands human development:

- as a sequential, step-by-step process
- as entailing the broad categories of childhood, adolescence, adulthood and aging

---

[1]"Youth," in *Merriam-Webster Online* <http://www.m-w.com/cgi-bin/dictionary?book=Dictionary&va=youth>.

[2]"Adolescence," in *Merriam-Webster Online* <http://www.m-w.com/cgi-bin/dictionary?book=Dictionary&va=adolescence>.

- as a process in stages that are hierarchical, moving from less complex processes to more complex processes
- as primarily tied to chronological age and physical maturation
- as possessing patterns that cannot be significantly altered within humans, who are more similar than dissimilar
- as a process affected but not controlled by the external environment, which may enable or hinder it
- as a process that allows a person to reconfigure, restructure, refashion and reconstruct some of the qualitative changes of earlier stages with each more advanced developmental stage[3]

ADOLESCENT DEVELOPMENT

Adolescence is generally divided into three stages. Each stage focuses on a primary life question and a primary emotional/psychological issue. Table 7.1 outlines these three stages and their related issues.[4]

Table 7.1. Adolescent Development

Stage	Age	Primary question	Primary issue
Early adolescence	11/12 to 13/14	Who am I?	Ego identity
Middle adolescence	13/14 to 17/19	Does life matter?	Autonomy
Late adolescence	17/19 to early 20s	Who am I in relation to others?	Mutuality and intimacy

Early Adolescence. The initial movement into adolescence occurs at between eleven or twelve and thirteen or fourteen years of age. Teenagers were not born teenagers. Adolescents are persons moving beyond child-

---

[3]These developmental assumptions are summarized from James C. Wilhoit and John M. Dettoni, *Nurture That Is Christian: Development Perspectives on Christian Education* (Grand Rapids: Baker, 1995), pp. 19-44; Mari Gonlag, "Developmental Tasks," in *Evangelical Dictionary of Christian Education*, ed. Michael J. Anthony (Grand Rapids: Baker, 2001), pp. 199-200.

[4]This section is greatly informed by "Who Are Youth? Development and Pastoral Perspectives," a lecture given by Dr. Harold Horell in *Youth and Young Adults* at Fordham University Graduate School of Religions and Religious Education, September 23, 2004; "Toward Christian Sexual Maturity: Growing in Wisdom, Age and Grace," a lecture given by Rev. Dr. John Cecero, *Pastoral Conference: Human Sexuality in the Roman Tradition,* at Fordham University Graduate School for Religion and Religious Education (GSRRE), October 28, 2004; Chap Clark, "The Changing Face of Adolescence: A Theological View of Human Development" in *Starting Right: Thinking Theologically about Youth Ministry,* ed. Kenda Creasy Dean, Chap Clark and Dave Rahn (Grand Rapids: Zondervan, 2001), 41-61.

hood who bring with them personal assets and liabilities from their previous stage of development.

Early adolescence is marked by clearly visible biological changes. Boys and girls begin to grow into young men and young ladies. Also, psychological changes are triggered by the biological changes. How adolescents view and understand their changing bodies will greatly determine how they view themselves. (This will be discussed in depth in chapter eight, "The Biology of Urban Youth.") This is where the church can play an important role in helping early adolescents develop a healthy understanding of the body and of the self. It is the time when teens begin to ask themselves the primal adolescent question, Who am I?

Finally, early adolescents also develop third-person perspective. That is, they now become much more concerned with how others view them: What does he think about me? What is she saying about me?

This is also when parents begin to lose their "coolness." Where one lives also reflects on how others may judge. Early adolescents may or may not want to bring their friends to their home depending on how it reflects on them. The way in which a teen dresses may also be confusing for parents. While an adolescent may look sloppy to a parent, this might be the exact look that the teenager is attempting to adopt. As of this writing, messy hair, ripped jeans, faded T-shirts and fitted jackets are cool. Puma and Converse sneakers (which were popular when I was a teenager in the 1970s) are now retro and very cool. In a few years, this look may be out of style. But if you wait long enough, based on fashion cycles, when these teenagers are in their middle-age years, that very style may become cool once again.

Of course, issues of sexuality are part of identity formation and biological changes. There is little more edifying than a youth ministry that provides a safe space for discussing these issues and nurtures a healthy Christian sexual awareness. There is little more damaging than a youth ministry that disallows a safe space for discussing these issues and nurtures unhealthy Christian sexual awareness. Again, this topic is much too broad to be discussed in any comprehensive way here. However, two developmental issues regarding sexual intimacy during early adolescence should be identified.

First, if sexual intimacy is experienced too early, it confounds and confuses the self-identity development. Early adolescents are beginning to develop a healthy self-identity. Sexual intimacy at this time tends to overload the identity-development process. Sexual intimacy is too complex an issue for adolescents who are just moving from childhood. Issues regarding sexuality are difficult for healthy adults to fully process and comprehend. Imagine how much more difficult they are for adolescents who are just beginning to make sense of life. Of course, this does not negate the importance of healthy sexual education and dialogue, which are essential.

Second, with sexual intimacy, the adolescent becomes too dependent on the other person too soon. How many times have we heard adolescent girls make statements such as, "I'll die if we can't stay together." Or, adolescent boys may say, "If I can't have you, no one will." These are statements that, if said by an adult, would sound adolescent. While healthy nonsexual relationships are important and essential, the sexually intimate dynamic tends to bind people in a way that is very difficult and complicated to separate without a great deal of emotional suffering and physical withdrawal. Again, as difficult and complicated as it is for adults to separate from or end a sexually intimate relationship, imagine how much more difficult and complex it is for adolescents.

Middle adolescence. From about thirteen or fourteen years old to seventeen or nineteen years old, middle adolescence is the complex and often painful heart of adolescence. Middle adolescence centers on the second separation-individuation phase.[5] Early adolescence begins the development of a personal identity as a young person separates from the roles and identity held as a child: Who am I? Middle adolescence begins a second separation—separation from roles and identity that are thought to be projected onto the adolescent from others: Who am I as a person? Does life matter?

While identity and individuation seem to be the key developmental issues of early adolescence, it is autonomy that now becomes paramount. Any parent or guardian who has raised an adolescent understands the often painful battles between teenage independence and parental oversight. This is often experienced when a parent still sees his or her adolescent son or daughter as a young child instead of as an adolescent who is moving

---

[5]See Chap Clark, "The Changing Face of Adolescence: A Theological View of Human Development," in *Starting Right: Thinking Theologically About Youth Ministry,* ed. Kenda Creasy Dean, Chap Clark and Dave Rahn (Grand Rapids: Zondervan, 2001), pp. 41-61.

away from young childhood roles, re-envisioning self-identity and wanting more autonomy. At this stage, the parent or guardian may take on a new role in the adolescent's life.

Late adolescence. From about seventeen/nineteen years old to early twenties, late adolescence marks the stage and process of moving from adolescence to young adulthood. While early adolescence is greatly informed by biology, the late adolescence is largely defined by culture. It is a time of social adjustment and the realization that, "I'm changing, but the world is not changing."

During late adolescence, one is better able to develop a sense of narrative coherence. When the adolescent is younger, he or she is unable to understand and put together, in an orderly fashion, his or her life story—a narrative coherence. As the adolescent matures, a personal story begins to develop and come together. This is also the time when the brain begins to develop in such a way that it can formulate more abstract thinking. It is no coincidence that college-age students question their faith, begin to change their thinking and are awakened to the wonders of life. They are like butterflies breaking forth from their adolescent cocoon. There is no need to fear this late adolescent and young adulthood stage. In fact, we should celebrate along with them.

This recognition of the passage from late adolescence to young adulthood highlights two important issues. First, it is vitally important to develop a young adult ministry separate from youth ministry. It has been my experience that this is particularly problematic in Latino churches in the urban context. It is not uncommon to have people in their mid-twenties to mid-thirties in youth ministry. A thirteen-year-old and a nineteen-year-old should not be with each other during certain youth ministry activities and discussions. Certain issues must be addressed in ways that are developmentally appropriate. Frankly, some youth ministries are too mature for their youth, while others are too immature for their youth.

Second, this underscores the importance of developing a theologically and emotionally healthy youth ministry. If a teenager has been exposed to an environment which is spiritually and emotionally healthy, then the late adolescent phase becomes a wonderful time of discovery rather than a stage for adults to fear.

During late adolescence, one redefines existing relationships and becomes open to developing new relationships for the first time. Late adolescents desire even more independence, while their parents are struggling with letting go of their young child and embracing their young adult son or daughter.

In many cultures today, the boundaries between late adolescence and young adulthood have become blurred. Adolescents are taking on adult roles earlier and earlier, yet settle on a career path (or marriage) later and later. Adolescents are also led to think about sexuality earlier and earlier, while the time of sexual-identity exploration is tending to become greater and greater (and marriage is being postponed later and later).

Therefore, the primary developmental question during the late adolescent stage tends to be, Who am I in relation to others? This emphasizes the developmental issues of mutuality and intimacy. This also seems to explain the late adolescent and young adult attraction to small groups, intimate gatherings and community.

HOW PSYCHOLOGY CAN HELP THE PROPHETIC YOUTH WORKER

- It helps the youth worker appreciate the dignity of each adolescent subgroup: early, middle and late.

- It helps the youth worker to become aware of the particular needs of each adolescent subgroup.

- Finally, it helps the youth worker to develop an age-appropriate youth ministry strategy. As previously mentioned, some youth ministries are too mature and others are too immature for their adolescents. An understanding of developmental stages helps the youth worker to more strategically and effectively minister to each group. While this may seem too complicated or unrealistic for some youth workers, it stresses the level of professionalism and training required of youth workers today to develop an effective youth ministry. I am aware that in many urban churches there are little money, few resources and few volunteers to expand the youth ministry. Youth workers, however, should do their best to add healthy Christian adults to their leadership team, then subdivide their youth ministry into groups of early, middle and late adolescents. If this is not immediately possible, then they should at least attempt to divide the youth ministry into two groups—ages eleven to fourteen (middle school) and fifteen to nineteen (high school). Even this simple separation will allow the youth worker to develop a more age-appropriate strategy.

BIBLICAL PERSPECTIVES ON DEVELOPMENTAL PSYCHOLOGY

Christian psychologist Larry Crabb presents four approaches to understanding the relationship between clinical and theological perspectives.[6]

Approach one: Theological perspective alone. This approach supposes that the only valid and acceptable perspective that one can have in order to understand human development is a solely biblical one.

Approach two: Clinical theology. This approach attempts to integrate both perspectives, but the clinical perspective over-psychologizes the theological perspective to such an extent that the theological perspective loses its authentic biblical dimension. Terms like *sin, redemption, grace, guilt* and *conviction* lose their Christian meaning.

Approach three: Clinical and theology perspectives unrelated. This approach supposes that both perspectives are legitimate, but that they are unrelated.

Approach four: Clinical and theological integration. This holistic approach acknowledges that all truth is God's truth. God is the author of all truth, whenever and from whatever source it comes. This approach also calls for wisdom, discernment and understanding. Therefore, this approach affirms the integration of the clinical and theological perspectives of human development, as long as it is consistent with biblical truth.

Prophetic youth workers accept the fourth approach—integration of clinical and theological perspectives. Psychology is a gift from God that enables us to better understand our thinking and our behavior. The Bible is filled with Scripture passages with developmental overtones.

We see the reasoning ability and appropriateness of each developmental stage. We also see the inappropriateness of an adult behaving as a child.

> When I was a child, I talked like a child, I thought like a child, I reasoned like a child. When I became a man, I put childish ways behind me. (1 Corinthians 13:11)

---

[6]Taken from Lawrence J. Crabb, *Effective Biblical Counseling: A Model for Helping Caring Christians Become Capable Counselors* (Grand Rapids: Zondervan, 1977); Duffy Robbins, *This Way to Youth Ministry: An Introduction to the Adventure* (Grand Rapids: Zondervan, 2004).

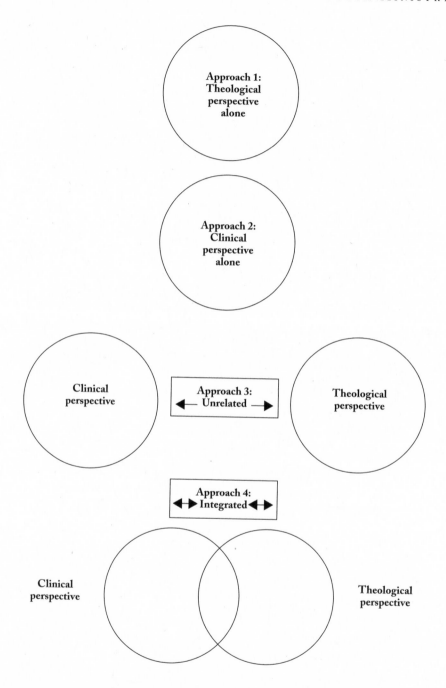

Figure 7.1. Approaches to understanding clinical and theological perspectives

We engage in appropriate interaction depending on each development stage.

> I gave you milk, not solid food, for you were not yet ready for it. Indeed, you are still not ready. (1 Corinthians 3:2)

We are exhorted to grow in the faith beyond elementary truths.

> In fact, though by this time you ought to be teachers, you need someone to teach you the elementary truths of God's word all over again. You need milk, not solid food! (Hebrews 5:12)

CHILDREN, FAITH AND DEVELOPMENTALISM

A critique of developmental psychology is its linear and phased understanding of human development. This leads one to believe that the older one gets, the more mature one becomes—hopefully. Life experience has shown, however, this is not always the case. I am familiar with teenagers and young adults who are more mature than middle-aged adults.

It is expected that the older one becomes, the more mature one becomes in faith development. While it is logical to assume that with developmental maturity and life experience come deeper awareness, increased knowledge and wisdom, the logic of God is quite different. As we have seen, the Scriptures do present an understanding of developmental growth. Yet it is quite interesting that, according to Jesus, spiritual growth for his disciples requires a return to childhood. Here lies the tension of Christian growth—to mature and grow on the one hand and to return to the simplicity and purity of childhood on the other. The Reverend Paul Dordal, a close friend, once said, "Perhaps what's wrong with the Church and the world is that we are actually too sophisticated. We have become so intelligent that we have lost our humility and simplicity. We rely on ourselves and our intelligence rather than relying on Jesus and the simple message of the Gospel. The gospel is too simple for the world and so [the world] rejects Jesus." Perhaps Paul is correct. While Jesus challenges his hearers to reject spiritual childishness, he encourages a return to spiritual childlikeness.

> And he said: "I tell you the truth, unless you change and become like little children, you will never enter the kingdom of heaven. Therefore, whoever humbles himself like this child is the greatest in the kingdom of heaven." (Matthew 18:3-4)

Jesus said, "Let the little children come to me, and do not hinder them, for the kingdom of heaven belongs to such as these." (Matthew 19:14)

At that time Jesus said, "I praise you, Father, Lord of heaven and earth, because you have hidden these things from the wise and learned, and revealed them to little children." (Matthew 11:25)

But when the chief priests and the teachers of the law saw the wonderful things he did and the children shouting in the temple area, "Hosanna to the Son of David," they were indignant.

"Do you hear what these children are saying?" they asked him.

"Yes," replied Jesus, "have you never read,

" 'From the lips of children and infants
you have ordained praise'?" (Matthew 21:15-16)

DANGERS OF DEVELOPMENTAL EXTREMISM

- Developmentalism may assume maturation is entirely linear. Adolescents grow and mature in different ways.

- Developmentalism may be too inclined to perceive adolescent development as staged or phased. Life is not always so planned and neat.

- Because of developmentalism's linear presentation, it does not view life as cyclical. Life is often a going forth and returning back, going forth and returning back. As clinical psychology has shown us, to address or uncover problems in the lives of adults, one must return to childhood. It is then that we can proceed with life.

- A misunderstanding of developmentalism may lead one to consider adolescents as incomplete or immature adults. This could not be further from the truth. Adolescence has a dignity in and of itself. Adolescents are no more incomplete adults than children are incomplete adolescents. Again, we must recognize and celebrate the dignity of each season of life.

8

The Biology of Urban Youth

This chapter will address three specific areas of biological concern: adolescent brain development, hormones and physical changes. There are many resources which address the issues of hormones and changes in the adolescent body. In my experience, most popular discussions regarding adolescent biology tend to focus on hormones, changes in the body and sex education. While these are certainly critical issues, the majority of this chapter will be dedicated to adolescent brain development.

BRAIN DEVELOPMENT AND ADOLESCENT BEHAVIOR

An early understanding of brain development was that most changes in the brain occurred during the first few years of life. In early childhood, even in the womb during the first nine months of life, there is a surge in production of gray cells. This gray matter is what gives us conscious thought and reason.[1] It is the "thinking" part of the brain. The cerebral cortex is the extensive outer layer of gray matter. It was previously believed that after three years there was little further brain development. We now know this is not true. Even though by the age of six 95 percent of the brain is the same size as the adult brain, it is still underdeveloped.

It is now recognized that during puberty the prefrontal cortex (PFC) goes through a second surge of production of these cells and thickening of the gray matter. This burst of neurons reaches to connect with other neu-

---

[1]For an introduction on brain research and adolescence, see David Walsh, *Why Do They Act That Way? A Survival Guide to the Adolescent Brain for You and Your Teen* (New York: Free Press, 2004).

rons. On the one hand, this discovery is revolutionary. It reveals that the adolescent brain is still undergoing changes. The thinking part of the brain is still developing—and the process is not yet complete. The adolescent PFC is still under construction and continues to develop into the early twenties. This would explain much of what is viewed as irrational adolescent behavior. This should also reassure the youth worker, and all adults, that adolescent behavior is only a season, albeit a challenging one.

On the other hand, this also highlights the stress that adolescents experience during this period. It explains, in part, the inner confusion adolescents often experience and are unable to articulate. During the time when teens are undergoing the challenges of puberty, chemical changes, hormonal changes and peer pressure, their PFC is fighting, adapting and trying to understand its environment. This also underscores the devastation that alcohol and drug use can have on this malleable and fragile adolescent brain during this phase of brain development.[2]

Much of our current understanding of brain development is rooted in the research of Jay N. Giedd. In 1999, Giedd published his landmark work "Brain Development During Childhood and Adolescence: A Longitudinal MRI Study."[3] Giedd studied 145 healthy boys and girls at the Child Psychiatry Branch of the National Institute of Mental Health. Over a two-year period, Giedd performed magnetic resonance imaging (MRI) on children and teens ranging from four to twenty-one years of age. While the language is technical, it is critical to read Giedd's insight in his own words.

> Pediatric neuroimaging studies, up to now, exclusively cross sectional, identify linear decreases in cortical gray matter and increases in white matter across ages 4 to 20. In this large scale longitudinal pediatric neuroimaging study, we confirmed linear increase in white matter, *but demonstrated nonlinear changes in cortical gray matter,* with a preadolescent increase followed by postadolescent decrease. These changes in cortical gray matter were regionally specific, with developmental curves for the frontal and parietal lobe peaking at about the age of 12 and for the temporal lobe at about

---

[2]See the video "Inside the Teenage Brain: An InterView with Dr. Jay Giedd," *Frontline,* January 31, 2002 <www.pbs.org/wgbh/pages/frontline/shows/teenbrain/interviews/giedd.html>.

[3]See Jay N. Giedd et al., "Brain Development During Childhood and Adolescence: A Longitudinal MRI Study," *Nature Neuroscience* 2 (1999): 861-63.

age 16, whereas *cortical gray matter continues to increase in the occipital lobe through age 20. . . .*

The absolute size of the cortical gray matter was approximately 10% larger in boys and peaked slightly earlier in girls, but the shapes of the curves were not significantly different between boys and girls. . . .

This MRI study demonstrates a preadolescent increase in cortical gray matter; this phenomenon was previously obscured, probably by the lack of longitudinal data. . . . *If the increase is related to a second wave of overproduction of synapses, it may herald a critical stage of development when the environment or activities of the teenager may guide selective synapse elimination during adolescence.*[4]

The prophetic youth worker should become familiar with basic human biology. In 2002, Britney Spears's hit single "I'm Not a Girl, Not Yet a Woman" reached the twenty-ninth spot on the billboard charts. This song struck a nerve with teenage girls, and appropriately so. Teenage girls, and boys, often feel in between. They cannot fully explain or understand their feelings, thoughts and changes. With the advent of puberty, there are rapid changes occurring that seem strange and confusing, especially for early adolescents. However, recent research on adolescent brain development has helped adults, youth workers and adolescents themselves to better understand why teens act the way they do.

Spears's song may also be appropriately translated, "I'm Not a Boy, Not Yet a Man." These words reflect not only adolescent developmental psychology, but adolescent developmental biology as well. This sense of in-between time is most helpful when trying to understand the adolescent brain. The adolescent brain is not a child's brain, not yet an adult brain.

BRAIN AND MIND

It is important to distinguish the brain from the mind. The brain is an organ. It is the control center of the central nervous system. The mind is the organized conscious and unconscious mental activity of the brain. The mind allows one to think, perceive, feel, will, remember and imagine. Yet, there is a correlation between the brain and the mind. When the brain is

---

[4]Ibid. (emphasis mine).

traumatized, injured or functioning poorly, it will directly affect a person's ability to think, reason, emote and remember. For example, schizophrenia, a brain disorder which usually emerges during late adolescence and young adulthood, can range symptomatically from hallucinations, delusions and thought disorder (positive symptoms) to flat affect, lack of pleasure in life and inability to initiate or sustain a planned activity (negative symptoms). Sadly, people with schizophrenia attempt suicide much more often than the general population. About 10 percent (especially younger adult males) succeed.[5] Presently, there is no cure. Treatment of the symptoms, however, is possible. This underscores the relationship between the brain and one's thinking and behavior. David Walsh explains this relationship in *Why Do They Act That Way?*

> The brain is the hardware. The mind is the software. Of course this metaphor gets complicated right away because in the case of the human brain the software—the mind—can actually affect the makeup of the hardware and vice versa.[6]

In *Hardwired Behavior,* Laurence R. Tancredi affirms the relationship between the brain and mind by applying it to moral reasoning. He writes,

> We are learning that social morality begins in the brain, for without the brain, there would be no concept of morality; the brain allows for interaction among individuals within the community, and this interaction leads to the construction of a framework for moral order.[7]

Immediately, one can see the direct relationship between the brain and behavior. It is important to note at this point that the adolescent brain is developmentally in between. Current brain research has established that the adolescent brain is not fully developed.[8] Therefore, if an adolescent behaves

---

[5]See "Schizophrenia," National Institute of Mental Health <http://www.nimh.nih.gov/publicat/schizoph.cfm>.

[6]Walsh, *Why Do They Act That Way?* p. 27.

[7]Laurence R. Tancredi, *Hardwired Behavior: What Neuroscience Reveals About Morality* (New York: Cambridge University Press, 2005), p. ix.

[8]This section on brain development is greatly informed by four sources: Walsh, *Why Do They Act That Way?;* Tancredi, *Hardwired Behavior;* the video "Inside the Teenage Brain"; "The Teenage Brain: A World of Their Own," *The Secret Life of the Brain* (New York: Thirteen/WNET; David Grubin Productions, 2001) <http://www.pbs.org/wnet/brain>. See also Giedd et al., "Brain Development During Childhood and Adolescence," pp. 861-63.

or thinks in ways that seem unreasonable—overly emotional, lacking judgment, careless, or without fear or sense of consequences—this may reflect the underdevelopment of the brain rather than moral or ethical failure.

Due to the nature and limitations of this book, an exhaustive examination of current adolescent brain research is not possible here. Nevertheless, I will highlight some of the major issues which, I believe, should be familiar to youth workers.

THE REPTILIAN BRAIN (OR THE BRAINSTEM)

Paul MacLean describes the human brain as a "triune brain," composed of three distinct brain systems functioning as one.[9] The first brain system is the brainstem. It is often referred to as the reptilian brain because it governs those aspects which are necessary and common among animals for physical survival. It is responsible for our unconscious physiological functions such as breathing, reproduction, heartbeat, circulation, digestion and involuntary fight-or-flight responses.[10]

THE EMOTIONAL BRAIN (OR THE LIMBIC SYSTEM)

The second brain system is the emotional brain.[11] MacLean refers to this as the limbic brain. *Limbic* comes from the Latin word *limbus*, "ring." The limbic brain system physically rings the brainstem. This is the seat of emotion. It is this part of the brain which deals directly with teen impulsiveness and anger.

The emotional brain has five limbic structures which are significant in understanding the adolescent brain.[12] (1) The *amygdala* is a little nut-shaped collection of brain cells which controls a full range of emotions, including anger, jealousy, embarrassment, affection and love. Its most significant emotion, however, is fear. When someone surprises you by jumping out from behind a corner, your immediate response is governed by the amygdala. The amygdala also plays a prominent role with boys and tes-

---

[9]Paul MacLean, *The Triune Brain in Evolution: Role in Paleocerebral Functions* (New York: Plenum, 1990). See also Walsh, *Why Do They Act That Way?* p. 29.

[10]MacLean, *Triune Brain in Evolution.*

[11]Tancredi, *Hardwired Behavior,* p. 34.

[12]This section is informed by Walsh, *Why Do They Act That Way?* p. 30, and Tancredi, *Hardwired Behavior,* pp. 34-37.

tosterone, especially with regard to sexual interest and aggression. This will be discussed more in depth in the section on hormones. (2) The *hippocampus* plays a role in remembering and memory. It complements the amygdala by linking the emotional response to memories, images and learning. It works to regulate the arousal of the emotions. The hippocampus is also involved in transforming new memories into long-term memories. In fact, it plays a prominent role with girls and estrogen, especially in the role of memory. This will be discussed more in depth in the section on hormones. Unfortunately, an adolescent's hippocampus can be significantly damaged by drinking and drug use. (3) The *anterior cingulated cortex (ACC)* deals with problem solving and uncertainty. As the brain's mediator, the ACC is involved with the prefrontal cortex because it is involved with uncertainty and decision making, as well as detecting conflict between plans and action. The ACC is also involved in emotional self-control, conflict resolution and error recognition. With regard to this important limbic component, Tancredi writes,

> The ACC dampens the effects of strong emotional reactions; it controls the effects of distress on the individual by reining in the amygdala to temper negative emotions. In doing so, the ACC provides for civilized discourse, conflict resolution, and fundamental human socialization.[13]

(4) The *hypothalamus* is the center of the endocrine or hormone system. It is the oldest of the limbic structures. The hypothalamus controls and regulates the arousal systems, such as those related to sex, food, consumption, aggression and rage. It also regulates heartbeat, blood pressure, temperature, thirst, hunger, hormone secretion and energy. The adolescent's raging hormones and sexual drive are directly associated with the hypothalamus. This will be discussed more in depth in the section on hormones. (5) The *ventral striatal (VS)* circuit is involved in the adolescent proclivity toward risky behavior. According to James M. Bjork, there are at least two views on this issue, as he has written in *Incentive-Elicited Brain Activation in Adolescents: Similarities and Differences from Young Adults*.

---

[13]Tancredi, *Hardwired Behavior*, p. 36.

One theory holds that risky behavior in adolescence results in part from a relatively overactive ventral striatal (VS) motivational circuit that readily energizes approach toward salient appetitive cues. However, other evidence fosters a theory that this circuit is developmentally underactive, in which adolescents approach more robust incentives (such as risk taking or drug experimentation) to recruit this circuitry.[14]

Regardless of perspective, it highlights the role VS plays in the lives of adolescent behavior. VS is also is involved in motivation. The underdeveloped VS in the adolescent brain may be the reason teens seem to lack drive. Teen laziness appears to be brain based.

THE THINKING BRAIN (OR THE PREFRONTAL CORTEX)

The third brain system is the cortex. The cortex makes up 80 percent of all brain mass. However, what is most significant in understanding the adolescent brain is the part of the cortex called the prefrontal cortex (PFC). The PFC, also referred to as the frontal cortex or the frontal lobes, is directly behind the forehead. It is the brain's chief executive officer. Walsh writes,

> The PFC regulates how the rest of the body and other parts of the brain functions. It is the decision maker, the planner that weighs the options that other parts of the brain present to it. The PFC is also one of the adolescent brain's major construction sites.[15]

In *The Executive Brain,* Elkhonon Goldberg writes, "the frontal lobes are the most uniquely human of all brain structures."[16] Tancredi expands this perspective even more dramatically.

> Indeed, these lobes have often been credited with empowering humanity to create civilizations containing art, science, culture, and social institutions. Thus it is within these lobes—in this area of the brain—that we find the seat of intellection, of cognitive functioning, of personality and identity, and of the integration of emotions and thought.[17]

---

[14]See James M. Bjork et al., "Incentive-Elicited Brain Activation in Adolescents: Similarities and Differences from Young Adults," *The Journal of Neuroscience* 24, no. 8 (2004): 1793-1802.
[15]Walsh, *Why Do They Act That Way?* p. 43.
[16]Elkhonon Goldberg, *The Executive Brain: Frontal Lobes and the Civilized Mind* (New York: Oxford University Press, 2001), p. 2.
[17]Tancredi, *Hardwired Behavior,* p. 38.

The PFC truly is the chief executive officer of the brain. It is responsible for motor control and movements and for the integration of stimuli in the thalamus, which relays information to the cerebral cortex for higher brain functions. It is connected to the emotional part of the brain (limbic system) and is directly related to the reptilian brain (the brainstem). Most importantly, it plays a major, perhaps the most significant, role in the thinking process.

This is the part of the brain that helps in making decisions, reasoning, judgment, self-control, planning ahead, organizing, solving problems, considering consequences and managing emotional impulses. Of particular importance to Christian youth workers, the PFC is also considered the brain's conscience and place of moral reasoning. It is in this part of the brain that one cognitively reflects on the mysteries of God and moral behavior.[18]

GENETICS AND EXPERIENCE

Two forces drive the wiring of the brain: genetics and experience.[19] Genes produce the DNA, the blueprint, needed to be a human being. The instructions encoded in the DNA determine which neurons connect with others and when. Genetics is referred to as *hard-wiring*, complemented by the *soft-wiring* shaped by life's experiences.[20]

This distinction between genetics and experience has often led to heated debates. Even moral development theories rooted in psychology also involve human experience. But, these distinctions are becoming less and less clear. Tancredi writes,

> This distinction between nature and nurture no longer seems relevant because of scientific discoveries. Basic human dynamics are being shown more and more to be based in biology.[21]

---

[18]See Andrew Newberg, Eugene D'Aquili and Vince Rause, *Why God Won't Go Away* (New York: Random House, 2002); Shankar Vedantam, "Tracing the Synapses of Spirituality," *Washington Post*, June 17, 2001, p. A01 <http://www.washingtonpost.com/ac2/wp-dyn/A8545-2001Jun15?language=printer>; Sharon Begley, "Religion and the Brain," *Newsweek*, May 7, 2001, p. 50 <https://notes.utk.edu/bio/greenberg.nsf/0/e938e40271ec394c85256a4a00626175?OpenDocument>.
[19]Walsh, *Why Do They Act That Way?* p. 28.
[20]Ibid.
[21]Tancredi, *Hardwired Behavior*, p. 20.

One may or may not agree with Tancredi's thesis. Certainly, as a Christian, I believe sin and grace play a role in human dynamics. Nevertheless, current brain research is increasingly showing greater neurological involvement in behavior.[22]

TWO FUNCTIONS DURING ADOLESCENT BRAIN DEVELOPMENT

There are two functions or processes that occur during adolescent brain development which are of particular significance for the urban youth worker: (1) the use-it-or-lose-it principle and (2) the window-of-opportunity principle.

The use-it-or-lose-it principle. As with any muscle, the brain needs to exercise to remain healthy and strong. The brain is essentially an electrical system.[23] The brain cells, called neurons, conduct the electrical signals. All neurons share a common structure. Each one has a cell body with an axon, a long cable, extending from it. Electrical impulses travel down the long cable to branches called dendrites, where the electrical impulses pass out of the cell through the branches, jump across a tiny gap and enter the branches of neighboring neurons.[24]

This is where the use-it-or-lose-it principle enters. Those cells (neurons) and connections that are used will survive and flourish. Those cells (neurons) that are *not* used will wither or die.[25] This is in keeping with the popular maxim, "The neurons that fire together wire together." Therefore, what an adolescent practices will reinforce certain parts of the brain. What is not utilized will weaken, and consequently fall off.

If a teenager is primarily exposed to academics, sports, healthy relationships, good manners, positive extracurricular activities, discipleship and positive affirmation, those are the cells (neurons) and connections that survive, flourish and are hard-wired. If a teenager is primarily exposed to hanging out, missing school, listening to songs with explicit language, watching music videos, lying on the couch, unhealthy relationships, curs-

---

[22]See any of the following for current neurological research: *Journal of Neuroscience, Brain Research Bulletin, Nature Neuroscience, Journal of Cognitive Neuroscience, Journal of Neurology* and *Neuron.*
[23]Walsh, *Why Do They Act That Way?* p. 27.
[24]Ibid.
[25]See "Inside the Teenage Brain: An Interview with Dr. Jay Giedd"; Walsh, *Why Do They Act That Way?* p. 32.

ing, playing violent video games and negative reinforcement, those are the cells (neurons) and connections that survive, flourish and are hard-wired.

Immediately, urban youth workers can see the challenges that confront them. How often have negatively hard-wired teens experienced rejection by churches that prefer positively hard-wired ones? Prophetic youth ministries are magnets for negatively hard-wired teens. Why? Because prophetic youth ministries intentionally welcome this type of adolescents. While prophetic youth ministries certainly don't tolerate disrespect, they tend to be much more patient and understanding. It is very likely that your youth ministries will be attended by teens who are negatively hard-wired. Prophetic youth ministries should be places that nurture healthy connections. For many urban youth, the prophetic youth ministry may be one of the few environments in which they receive positive affirmation.

Understanding the development of negatively hard-wired adolescents should be helpful to urban youth workers in two ways. First, the urban youth worker should be patient. You cannot undo, in a short period of time, the damage done to an adolescent who has received years of negative reinforcement. It may take years to loosen and rewire that negative hard-wiring. A youth worker may never see the results of the seeds of love planted in the lives of these teens. Second, the urban youth worker should experience a sense of relief from placing unrealistic burdens on themselves and expecting to reach unrealistic goals.

This process is also called *blossoming and pruning*. A helpful metaphor in regards to blossoming and pruning is, "The brain is like a tree." The tree has branches. Some branches are strengthened and survive. Other branches that are weakened begin to wither and are pruned. Life experiences cause the neurons to fire. Those branch connections bridging one cell to another get stronger. This is known as *blossoming*. The branches that that do not fire and connect will eventually shrink, wither and disappear. This is known as *pruning*.[26]

One of the ways in which the adolescent brain decides which cells and connections to strengthen and keep and which ones to eliminate and prune

---

[26]Walsh, *Why Do They Act That Way?* p. 33.

is based on the activities in which the adolescent is presently engaged. Giedd explains:

> The brain is searching and asking, "What am I going to need to be good at to survive in this environment?" And, the way it figures that out is by examining, "What am I doing now?"[27]

Therefore, what an adolescent practices will reinforce certain connections in the brain. What is not utilized will wither and die. This prompts the question, In what activities is the adolescent presently involved? Are they positive activities or negative activities? Once again, if the life experiences or practices of an adolescent are primarily negative, the positive connections necessary for a normal and healthy life begin to wither and die.

The window-of-opportunity principle. In 1981 David Hubel and Torsten Wiesel won the Nobel Prize for Medicine for years of work demonstrating the use-it-or-lose-it principle and the blossoming-and-pruning principle. In one of their early experiments, Hubel and Wiesel sutured the eyelids of newborn kittens. The kittens were well cared for in every other way. Three months later, the sutures were removed. Even though the eyes of the kittens were intact, the animals were blind. And, they remained blind for the rest of their lives. Walsh explains,

> Because the brain cells that would have been dedicated to vision had not been used, they had withered away or had become dedicated to some other useful function by the time the kittens could open their eyes.[28]

The window of opportunity for these kittens to hard-wire their neurons and connections for vision was open during the early months. But the window of opportunity was lost. The neurons and connections dedicated for vision were no longer available.

Research shows that in the first three years of human life the window of opportunity is open widest for phonetic awareness.[29] Urban youth workers know quite well teens exposed to and speaking words and phrases which are grammatically incorrect, street slang or inappropriate language. If these

---

[27]"The Teenage Brain: A World of Their Own," episode three of the PBS series *The Secret Life of the Brain*, prod. David Grubin, 2002 <www.pbs.org/wnet/brain/episode3/index.html>.

[28]Walsh, *Why Do They Act That Way?* p. 32.

[29]Ibid., pp. 34-35.

teens have been exposed to this type of speech for most of their lives, the window of opportunity to undo this hard-wiring may not be totally closed, but, as so many of us know, it will certainly be a long and difficult journey to keep open and rewire. This is demonstrated in the movie *Akeelah and the Bee.*

Akeelah, a precocious African American middle-schooler, who doesn't want her friends to discover her above-average academic abilities, agrees to participate in a regional spelling bee. She reluctantly consents to be coached by Dr. Larabee, an English professor. Dr. Larabee, also African American, demands nothing less than excellence and also will not allow her to speak slang. From this point on Akeelah, slowly and with occasional relapses, begins to rewire her language. As her vocabulary expands and use of language improves, Akeelah is transformed as well.

The adolescents who enter through the doors of a youth ministry bring with them all the past experiences hard-wired during the window of opportunity. This further underscores the critical importance of creating an environment of love and acceptance, of forgiveness and redemption. Teens should certainly respect the values and boundaries of the Christian faith. Yet, adolescents who have been negatively hard-wired should also experience the immense joy of healing found in the Christian faith. As Walsh reinforces, "Whatever happens while the window is open wires the brain."[30]

Putting it all together. The preceding discussion should make clear the value of understanding brain development. This is especially true with regard to the adolescent brain. Walsh summarizes,

> Until recently researchers believed that all . . . of these key developmental processes were completed by the time a boy or girl reached puberty. . . . [However] these vital processes continue well into adolescence. In fact, key brain areas undergo their blossoming and pruning periods *only* during adolescence. Further, the corpus callosum, which connects the right and left hemispheres, is still undergoing major construction from childhood into adolescence. The myelination process in certain parts of the teen brain actually *increases* by 100 percent from the beginning of adolescence to the end . . . Adolescents' developmental windows relate to the wiring of impulse con-

---

[30]Ibid., p. 36.

trol, relationships and communication. That's why we need to pay attention when an adolescent spends hours playing violent video games while his window of opportunity to develop healthy relationships is open wide. It also makes sense to encourage adolescents to get involved with service projects and volunteer opportunities while major brain circuits related to social relationship are blossoming and pruning.[31]

THE ADOLESCENT MORAL BRAIN

Is there a biology of morality? In 2004, Joshua Greene published his well-known study, "The Neural Bases of Cognitive Conflict and Control in Moral Judgment." Greene established that for decades, "traditional theories of moral psychology emphasized reasoning and 'higher cognition,' while more recent research emphasizes the role of emotions." In response to this research, he studied forty-one participants who responded to moral dilemmas while having their brains scanned using MRIs. He presented them with moral dilemmas, most notably the crying baby dilemma.

> Enemy soldiers have taken over your village. They have orders to kill all remaining civilians. You and some of your townspeople have sought refuge in the cellar of a large house. Outside, you hear the voices of soldiers who have come to search the house for valuables. Your baby begins to cry loudly. You cover his mouth to block the sound. If you remove your hand from his mouth, his crying will summon the attention of the soldiers who will kill you, your child, and the others hiding in the cellar. To save yourself and the others, you must smother your child to death. Is it appropriate for you to smother your child in order to save yourself and the other townspeople?[32]

Greene observed an increased spike in the anterior cingulated cortex (ACC), the part of the emotional brain which deals with problem solving and conflict resolution. This is the part of the brain which is considered the mediator.

Greene also observed that those respondents who chose to smother the baby had increased activity in the prefrontal cortex and the inferior parietal

---

[31]Ibid., p. 37.
[32]Joshua Greene et al., "The Neural Bases of Cognitive Conflict and Control in Moral Judgment," *Neuron* 44 (October 14, 2004): 389-400.

cortex, which are a part of the thinking brain or the rationale cognitive aspect of the brain. An interviewer reports that "in those who chose not to kill the baby, Greene says, it's possible to infer that, 'their response is driven by that emotional intuition.'"[33]

However, in *all* respondents, there was increased activity in the amygdala, which deals with the full range of emotions, most significantly fear.

> "Indeed there is this conflict between at least one response which we think is the emotional response, and this other response that we think is the cognitive cost-benefit analysis response," Greene says.
>
> Most likely, these results can be traced to "at least two different processes that are at work in moral judgment. We have intuitive emotional sort of responses that give us a quick sort of flash, a sense of, 'That's wrong' . . . and a slower, more reflective way of thinking of things, where we can conscientiously apply a moral rule or we can think about things in a more actuarial way, like an accountant adding up costs and benefits in deciding what to do."[34]

Greene's report of his research dramatically underscores the relationship between the brain and moral living. This brain-based moral connection may also be seen in three of the traditional deadly sins. First, gluttony may involve two brain systems: the system that sends hunger and satiation (satisfaction) messages and the system associated with reward circuits. The latter system is associated with the reward circuits involved in addiction to drugs, such as cocaine, heroin and marijuana. Second, sloth is closely aligned with depression. This may be connected to lower levels of several major neurotransmitters, including serotonin, dopamine and norepinephrine. Finally, lust is neurologically related to the hypothalamus. For boys, naturally, it is also connected with testosterone. Extreme behaviors seem to be related to addictive propensities in the brain. Also, people with minimal or overactive sexual desires may experience lesser or greater testosterone levels or other hormones.[35]

---

[33]Stacey Young, "Moral Dilemma," *ScienCentral News*, July 8, 2005 <www.sciencentral.com/articles/view.php3?type=article&article_id=218392590>.
[34]Ibid.
[35]Tancredi, *Hardwired Behavior*, p. 10.

Here lies the challenge. How does an urban youth worker develop adolescents in Christlike maturity in an environment seductively, and not so subtly, tempting and alluring them into negative hard-wiring situations and connections? Some of the most courageous and prophetic people I have met in urban ministry are the faithful and determined youth workers who through prayer, hard work and God's leading are trying to keep open the adolescent window of opportunity, hoping the Holy Spirit will prune and transform the negative hard-wiring in teens. There is no one model or easy solution. However, I do believe God is seeking well-trained and informed prophetic youth workers to create and nurture positive environments and connections so adolescent brains will be sensitized and blossom to the life-giving energy of the Holy Spirit.

As Christians, we recognize the reality of sin. It permeates all things; having entered into the world through the fall of Adam, it brings death to all people. When adolescents, like all people, sin, it still reflects the sinful nature of humanity. And, our hope is "that, just as sin reigned in death, so also grace might reign through righteousness to bring eternal life through Jesus Christ our Lord" (Romans 5:21). Nevertheless, we cannot deny the current research on brain development and its findings on how the brain can trigger certain moral behavior.

Tancredi aptly writes,

> Being moral, therefore, isn't easy. This is why moral training—early and often—is essential. Our brain structures are not immutable; they are susceptible to change for the better and change for the worse. What's important is what happens deep down at the level of the neuron—in a process called *neuroplasticity*. By neuroplasticity we mean the ability of neurons at the synapses to forge new connections, thereby essentially bringing about a rewiring of the brain.[36]

The prophetic youth ministry should be a place of positive spiritual neuroplasticity. It should help urban youth forge new spiritual connections, bringing about a rewiring of the brain, leading toward a transformation of the mind.

---

[36]Ibid., p. 43.

HORMONES AND THE ADOLESCENT BODY

Hormones are chemicals that move into the body fluid after they are made by a cell or group of cells. They affect other cells or tissues. Hormones are part of the endocrine system, one of the body's main systems for communicating, controlling and coordinating the body's work. The endocrine glands consist of the thymus, testes, ovaries, thyroid glands, adrenal glands, parathyroid glands, pancreas and kidney. Three endocrine glands are located in the brain. They are the pituitary, hypothalamus and pineal glands. Together, the hormone system and the nervous system make up the neuroendocrine system.[37]

Puberty. At the beginning of puberty, the hypothalamus sends a message to the pituitary gland to increase production of certain hormones because the body is ready to become an adult. Scientists have identified almost fifty different types of hormones.[38] I will focus on three main hormones: testosterone, estrogen and progesterone.

Hormones and boys. For boys, the primary hormone is testosterone. Testosterone triggers physical changes, such as dramatic growth and sudden voice changes. Adolescents can have five to seven surges of testosterone per day during the course of puberty.[39] By the end of adolescence, boys can have 1,000 percent of the amount of testosterone in their bodies that they had before puberty. Boys also have twenty times more testosterone than girls have at the same age.[40]

Testosterone also affects the brain, especially the amygdala. The amygdala, which is the seat of fear and aggression, has receptor sites for testosterone. Therefore, during puberty the amygdala is overstimulated. This triggers surges of anger, sexual interest, dominance and territoriality. It also explains the natural aggression of teenage boys. And, because testosterone is geared toward immediate tension release, adolescent boys are prone to follow any impulse that might release stress.[41]

Youth workers should be patient with adolescent boys' tendencies to-

---

[37]"The Endocrine System," The Hormone Foundation <www.hormone.org/endo101>.
[38]Walsh, *Why Do They Act That Way?* p. 61.
[39]Ibid., p. 62.
[40]Ibid.
[41]Ibid.

ward impulsivity and rough play. Yet, they also have to ensure that the boys don't hurt themselves or others. Youth ministries should incorporate programs and activities which allow boys to release their overstimulation in healthy and positive ways. This is especially true in the urban context where inner-city neighborhoods do not have sufficient parks, playgrounds or recreational centers allowing adolescent boys and girls to healthily release this naturally built up tension and overstimulation. I suspect that much of adolescent at-risk behavior may be the result of teens inappropriately releasing their tension and overstimulation in negative ways due to a lack of community support outlets.

Boys should be cautioned about being overly aggressive with others and respectful of those who are weaker. They should be taught about respecting and protecting girls. In particular, boys should not physically threaten or impose their natural aggressive tendency onto girls. Finally, it is important that boys be taught to appreciate and better understand adolescent girls' natural expressive and sharing tendencies.

Hormones and girls. Females have testosterone in their bloodstream produced by the adrenal glands, but at much lower levels than men.[42] For girls, there are two important hormones, estrogen and progesterone. As testosterone does for boys, estrogen triggers changes in girls. These changes include the development of breasts, widening of the pelvis and the beginning of the menstrual cycle. Estrogen also affects the brain. For girls, the primary receptor sites for estrogen are in the hippocampus. The hippocampus is the memory center, which explains why girls tend to have advantages over boys with regard to academic tasks requiring memory.[43]

Progesterone is produced primarily by the ovaries. It plays a crucial role in the normal menstrual cycle and in pregnancy. Progesterone helps to prepare the lining of the uterus to accept a fertilized egg but will cease production if the egg is not fertilized. Menstruation will follow.[44]

---

[42]Helen Fisher, *Why We Love: The Nature and Chemistry of Romantic Love* (New York: Holt, 2004), pp. 82-83.

[43]Walsh, *Why Do They Act That Way?* p. 63.

[44]"Progesterone," Women's Health, WebMD <http://women.webmd.com/Women-Medical-Reference/Progesterone-15286>; Kathy René Harris, "The Effects That the Following Hormones (Tes-tosterone, Estrogen, and Progesterone) Have on the Human Body," Yale-New Haven Teachers Institute <www.yale.edu/ynhti/curriculum/units/1988/5/88.05.04.x.html#p>.

Neurotransmitters. Estrogen and progesterone have a powerful influence over neurotransmitters, chemical substances that transmit messages from one nerve cell to another.[45] The primary neurotransmitters for adolescents are norepinephrine, dopamine and serotonin.

Norepinephrine is the energy neurotransmitter. It prepares the body for its fight-or-flight response. It is also important for memory. Dopamine is the feel-good neurotransmitter. When a person is attracted to someone or something, the levels of dopamine increase. One of the reasons drugs and alcohol are so addictive is because they can cause a surge in dopamine in the brain. Certain drugs, like cocaine and heroin, have been known to increase dopamine levels *above* orgasm levels.[46] Finally, serotonin is the neurotransmitter that stabilizes moods. In proper amounts, it helps us to feel relaxed and confident. A lack of serotonin can cause depression or aggression. Antidepressant drugs such as Prozac and Xanax increase levels of serotonin.[47]

Throughout puberty and into adulthood, the balance between estrogen and progesterone fluctuates during a woman's menstrual cycle. As the level of one hormone shifts, so does the level of the other. Because these hormones have such a powerful influence over the neurotransmitters, fluctuating hormone levels can lead to dramatic and sudden mood swings in girls. Estrogen also influences reactions to stress, sex drive and appetite.[48]

Youth workers, especially male youth workers, should be sensitive to the natural, yet often frustrating and confusing, hormonal fluctuations adolescent girls experience. Youth ministries should also incorporate activities which allow girls safe space to discuss these issues in healthy and positive ways. Adolescent girls should also be taught to respect adolescent boys and to understand their aggressive or rough tendencies.

A MALE BRAIN AND A FEMALE BRAIN?

The brain has two sides. The left hemisphere is the more analytical, thinking and linear side. This left hemisphere is engaged in math, language,

---

[45]"Neurotransmitter," in *Merriam-Webster Online* <www.m-w.com/dictionary/neurotransmitter>.
[46]"The Teenage Brain: A World of Their Own."
[47]Walsh, *Why Do They Act That Way?* pp. 63-64.
[48]Ibid., p. 64.

writing and reading. The right side is the more abstract, intuitive and visual side. The right hemisphere is engaged in listening to music, daydreaming and imagining. Clearly, we need both sides of the brain. While the left side departmentalizes, the right side synergizes.[49]

During infancy, the brain is undergoing its first major period of development. For girls, the left hemisphere of the brain develops before the right hemisphere. Language is centered in the left hemisphere. This seems to explain why girls master language earlier and more fluently than boys do.[50]

For boys, the right hemisphere of the brain develops before the left hemisphere. Spatial thinking is centered in the right hemisphere. This seems to explain why boys tend to do better in navigation and mental rotation tasks.[51]

The corpus callosum, the bridge of nerve fibers between the right and left hemispheres of the brain, tends to be thicker in the female brain. This suggests that women have an advantage in linking the analytical and verbal left brain with the intuitive right brain. When performing identical activities, brain scans show that men tend to focus their brain activity in one hemisphere or the other.[52]

In his neurological research, Simon Baron-Cohen presents a scientific approach to the differences between men and women. He distinguishes the female's more "empathic brain" from the male's more "systematizing brain."[53] According to Baron-Cohen, the empathic

Questions to Ponder

Prophetic youth ministries should be sensitive to both the empathic and the systematizing brain functions. Youth workers should also evaluate their personal leadership styles. Do you tend to be overly empathic at the expense of systematizing? Do you tend to be overly systematizing at the expense of empathy? If you are male, are you sensitive to adolescent girls and the way they think and cognitively process? If you are female, are you sensitive to adolescent boys and the way they cognitively process?

---

[49]Ibid., p. 31.
[50]Ibid., p. 97.
[51]Ibid., pp. 97-98.
[52]Ibid., p. 98.
[53]Simon Baron-Cohen, *The Essential Difference: The Truth About the Male and Female Brain* (New York: Basic Books, 2003), pp. 26-27.

brain is more subjective and has the capacity to comprehend, to feel the other person's position. The systematizing brain is more objective and focuses on systems, understanding how these work and how to construct them. Of course, changes in circumstances and experience can nurture and develop both sides of the brain. For example, a women who becomes a supervisor will develop her systematizing functions. Conversely, a man who is placed in a caretaking role will develop his empathic functions.

LOVE, SEX AND ADOLESCENTS

Adolescence begins with puberty. During puberty, the body becomes capable of reproduction. For girls, hormonal development begins as early as eight to nine years and as late as twelve to thirteen years. For boys, hormonal development begins as early as nine to ten years and as late as thirteen to fourteen years.[54]

During this time, adolescents produce a group of hormones called androgens, traditionally considered male hormones. But they are also crucial to women in developing strong muscles and bones, positive protein balance, and sexual desire. Androgens are sex hormones produced by the ovaries and adrenal glands for women and by the testes for men.[55]

As these increase, especially DHEA (dehydroepiandrosterone), boys and girls begin to experience their first crush. This is the beginning of real sexual awakening. For boys, the rapid development of the INAH-3 (the third interstitial nucleus of the anterior hypothalamus), which controls and regulates the arousal systems, overwhelms any thoughts of study, chores or prayer.[56] The combination of this maturing INAH-3 and the surges in testosterone naturally leads to sexual fantasies and desires. Levels of dopamine, the feel-good hormone, also increase.

The hypothalamus also drives the hormone levels that are responsible for sexual awakening in adolescent girls. Testosterone is present in both boys and girls. Although the levels are much higher in boys, testosterone

---

[54]Steven Gerali, "Sexuality, Adolescent," in *Evangelical Dictionary of Christian Education*, ed. Michael J. Anthony (Grand Rapids: Baker, 2001), p. 630.

[55]Walsh, *Why Do They Act That Way?* p. 118; see "Androgens in Women," Women's Health Program, Monash University <http://womenshealth.med.monash.edu.au/documents/androgens-in-women .pdf#search='androgens%20and%20women'>.

[56]Walsh, *Why Do They Act That Way?* p. 118.

provides the sex drive for both. According to Walsh, "Because of their testosterone surges, adolescent boys tend to view girls as sexual objects. Adolescent girls are more prone to focus on the relational aspects of sexual attraction, such as spending time together and talking."[57]

In "The Neural Basis of Romantic Love," Andreas Bartels and Semir Zeki report their brain studies of young people in love.[58] When the young persons thought about their loves, four separate areas of their brains became very active. Two were in the cortex, and the other two were deeper in the brain. Interestingly, the prefrontal cortex, the thinking brain, was inactive. This seems to indicate that when people are in love, they are not using the rationale aspect of their brain.

It is important for youth workers and adults to accept that these sexual feelings are not only normal, but they are neurologically wired and inevitable. Great caution should be taken not to morally shame adolescents for certain emotions and neurological impulses which are normal. However, also unacceptable is being silent, acting silly or being self-righteous about the subject. Christian youth workers have the important and difficult task of balancing compassion and understanding for the powerful and primal adolescent sexual urges with teaching the biblical understanding of God's design for human sexuality and its parameters for sexual behavior.

Kenda Creasy Dean's insights on adolescent passion and youth ministry in *Practicing Passion* seem both helpful and apropos in this regard.

> If adolescence and Christianity are both so full of passion, then why aren't young people flocking to the church? Maybe it is because the church, like the greeting card industry, has largely sanitized love of suffering, leaving Christianity with a mealy-mouthed niceness that fails to ring true to young people who know in their bones that love and heartache go together.[59]
>
> The mark of true Christianity, therefore, is love suffering: love that does not suffer—love that is reasonable, that can be explained by reflection—is a sham. The truth of divine love lies in its unreasonableness.[60]

---

[57]Ibid.

[58]Andreas Bartels and Semir Zeki, "The Neural Basis of Romantic Love," *Neuro Report* 11(2000): 3829-34.

[59]Kenda Creasy Dean, *Practicing Passion: Youth and the Quest for a Passionate Church* (Grand Rapids: Eerdmans, 2004), p. 6.

[60]Ibid., p. 65.

HOW BIOLOGY CAN HELP THE PROPHETIC YOUTH WORKER

- It helps the youth worker become more patient with adolescent behavior.
- It helps the youth worker better understand adolescent mood swings.
- It helps the youth worker better understand adolescent sexuality.
- It helps the youth worker better understand adolescent boys' natural tendency toward aggression.
- It helps the youth worker better understand adolescent girls' natural tendency toward language.
- It helps the youth worker better understand the relationship between adolescent biology and moral behavior.
- It helps the youth worker appreciate the mystery and complexity of the human body.
- It helps the youth worker better understand the relationship between the brain and the mind.
- It helps the youth worker appreciate the contributions of science.
- It helps the youth worker to better understand how boys and girls think similarly and differently.
- It helps the youth worker to demystify puberty and sexual behavior.
- It helps to remind the youth worker that the brain of a physically mature teenager is still developing.
- It helps the youth worker to better understand himself or herself.

BIBLICAL PERSPECTIVES ON BIOLOGY

Perhaps the greatest theological Christian truth that reflects a spirituality of biology is the incarnation. The incarnation is the mystery of God becoming enfleshed as a person. While, admittedly, the conception of Jesus was transbiological, conceived by the power of the Holy Spirit (Luke 1:26-38), his gestation, birth, life and death were lived out within the laws of biology.

In the story of the Last Supper, the night before his crucifixion, Jesus took a sacred Jewish ritual and made spiritual-biological connections between himself and his followers. There are many names for this Christian ritual: Holy Eucharist, Holy Communion, the Lord's Supper, the Breaking of the Bread and others.

> And he took bread, gave thanks and broke it, and gave it to them, saying, "This is my body given for you; do this in remembrance of me."
>
> In the same way, after the supper he took the cup, saying, "This cup is the new covenant in my blood, which is poured out for you." (Luke 22:19-20)

As we have read, the hippocampus plays a most significant role in remembering and memory. It complements the amygdala by linking the emotional response to memories, images and learning. It works to regulate the arousal of the emotions. In the story of the Last Supper, there are two spiritual-biological issues. First, Jesus incarnates his divine personhood into the very bread which he invites us to eat. Second, Jesus invites us to activate our hippocampus and remember him in the act of the Communion. Therefore, the very act of Communion is both a personal spiritual-neurological activation and a communal spiritual-bodily exercise. It is the remembering of a past event while making it effective in the present. The body of Christ gathers to remember and partake in the body of Christ.

Brain research highlights the neurological influences on one's behavior. These influences may be lesser or greater depending on genetics and circumstances. Those with significant brain damage are certainly struggling with painful realities. Yet, for the overwhelming majority of us, God challenges us to confront our negative hard-wiring. Paul writes,

> "Everything is permissible for me"—but not everything is beneficial. "Everything is permissible for me"—but I will not be mastered by anything. "Food for the stomach and the stomach for food"—but God will destroy them both. The body is not meant for sexual immorality, but for the Lord, and the Lord for the body. By his power God raised the Lord from the dead, and he will raise us also. Do you not know that your bodies are members of Christ himself? Shall I then take the members of Christ and unite them with a prostitute? Never! Do you not know that he who unites himself with a prostitute is one with her in body? For it is said, "The two will become one flesh." But he who unites himself with the Lord is one with him in spirit.
>
> Flee from sexual immorality. All other sins a man commits are outside his body, but he who sins sexually sins against his own body. Do you not know that your body is a temple of the Holy Spirit, who is in you, whom you have

received from God? You are not your own; you were bought at a price. Therefore honor God with your body. (1 Corinthians 6:12-20)

This Scripture passage addresses several moral issues. But three things Paul mentions are especially important to the real-life biological struggles of negative hard-wiring. First, not everything is beneficial. While our neurological wiring may desire something, this something may not necessarily be beneficial to our lives. Second, do not be mastered by anything. Any person who has attempted to stop using cigarettes, alcohol, drugs or any other addictive behavior, whether material or behavioral, understands the pain of withdrawal. The addict is enslaved to the addiction. God desires us to be free. Keep in mind, this addictive hard-wiring may not necessarily be a chemical substance. For example, try not using a cell phone, iPod, television or computer for one week. Do you experience withdrawal?

Finally, your body is a temple of the Holy Spirit. This underscores that we are made in the image of God. Sin has undoubtedly permeated our total being and all of creation. Sin has and continues to hard-wire our thinking and influences our behavior in ways that do not please God. But, we are reminded that we were "bought at a price" (1 Corinthians 6:20). Our brains and our bodies should not be enslaved to sin. Rather, our bodies should honor God. This is reinforced in Romans,

> Therefore do not let sin reign in your mortal body so that you obey its evil desires. Do not offer the parts of your body to sin, as instruments of wickedness, but rather offer yourselves to God, as those who have been brought from death to life; and offer the parts of your body to him as instruments of righteousness. (Romans 6:12-13)

DANGERS OF BIOLOGICAL EXTREMISM

- Biological extremism may rationalize religious experience as a brain phenomenon and deny the existence of God.
- Biological extremism may reduce the power of sin to a neurological or chemical imbalance.
- Biological extremism may rationalize all immoral behavior as neurologically based without personal moral culpability.
- Biological extremism may dismiss spiritual activity and even oppression

observed in an adolescent as nothing more than typical brain dysfunction.

- Biological extremism may justify and affirm sexual behavior outside of the biblical understanding of God's design and parameters.

- At its most extreme, it can lead a person to denying the existence of God by reducing the mystical experience to a neurological prefrontal function.

- A final danger of biological extremism is the tendency or possibility to resign oneself to perpetual negative behavior by rationalizing that this is the way one is hard-wired. It is always difficult to deny oneself something that one desires but is harmful. Our brain may decide that the struggle is irrational. Yet, this is what God demands: to sacrifice ourselves for God and offer him ourselves as instruments of righteousness. This will certainly require sacrifice and spiritual rewiring.

> Do not conform . . . to the pattern of this world, but be transformed by the renewing of your mind. Then you will be able to test and approve what God's will is—his good, pleasing and perfect will. (Romans 12:2)

9

The Sociology and Anthropology of Urban Youth

The prophetic youth worker should become familiar with basic sociology because prophetic theology addresses the contextual issues of youth ministry. It has been my experience that most urban youth ministries spend little time examining their ministry context sociologically. They simply go right into the theological aspect of youth ministry, providing the standard religious services without analyzing their socioeconomic context.

One of the most powerful ways to implement sociology in youth ministry is through the use of what nonprofit guru Peter Drucker calls the "Environmental Scan."[1] An environmental scan is a critical survey of an organization and designated area. This is very popular in church planting theory; a demographic study of one's community allows one to become more effective in ministry.

The New York City-based Latino Leadership Circle sponsors an excellent program called the Urban Youth Leadership Training Program. This program offers a training session entitled "Community Mapping," which is dedicated to helping urban youth workers more strategically understand their community. During this session, urban leaders are taught how to better analyze and understand the groups and institutions of their respective areas and how to develop working relationships with them.

Whether called the "environmental scan" or "community mapping," the purpose is the same—to better understand your ministry context. The na-

---

[1]See Peter F. Drucker, *The Drucker Foundation Self-Assessment Tool: Participant Workbook* (Hoboken, N.J.: Wiley, 1998).

ture of context, however, is not simply to familiarize oneself with community statistics in order to minister more effectively, although this is important. More importantly, it is a way to better understand the people that God has placed in a particular area. One may have a desire to minister to a certain group of people, but God may have brought a different group of people to our doors. This is an area where the field of youth ministry also fails. While the field may believe in contextualization in theory, based on its resources and writings it tends to focus on generic youth culture, which is not always consistent or relevant to the sociological realities of the urban youth context.

It is essential that the prophetic youth worker study and develop a community demographic profile. In the profile, certain data should be included: population figures, racial and ethnic groups, employment, poverty, housing, crime statistics and census tracts. Let us examine more in depth Manhattan Community District Eleven, New York City. This district includes East Harlem, Spanish Harlem and El Barrio and will be referred to simply as East Harlem.

EAST HARLEM PROFILE

- The mainland area of East Harlem covers approximately 946 acres or approximately 1.5 square miles.[2]
- The total population of East Harlem is 117,743 according to the 2000 census. This is a 6.6 percent population increase since 1990 and reverses the declining trend of previous decades.[3]
- In terms of racial/ethnic composition, of the total population in 2000, 55 percent of the residents were Hispanic. Blacks/African Americans made up the second largest group at 33 percent, followed by whites, who total 7 percent. Foreign-born residents constitute 21 percent of the population.[4]

---

[2]Community Board Eleven—Manhattan, "Statement of District Needs Fiscal Year 2007," The City of New York <www.cb11m.org/html/info/files/Statement%20FY07.pdf>.

[3]Please note that immigrants historically are leery of disclosing information to governmental agencies, particularly in regard to census matters. Therefore, based on the influx of immigrants into East Harlem, one can reasonably infer that the population figures are actually greater than reported.

[4]"Community Health Profile: East Harlem," New York City Department of Mental Health, 2006; <www.nyc.gov/html/doh/downloads/pdf/data/2006chp-303.pdf>.

- Of the total population, 28 percent are under the age of eighteen. Of this group, 57 percent are Hispanic and 36 percent are black/African American.

- Of the adult residents over eighteen years of age, the largest age group is between twenty-five and forty-four—31 percent.

- There are a total of 43,318 households in East Harlem. Of these households, 67 percent are unmarried. Only 33 percent are married-couple families with or without children.[5]

- Thirty-eight percent of East Harlem adults live in poverty, compared to 21 percent throughout New York City.[6] The median household income is $21,480, compared to the median income of Manhattan of $47,030.[7] Thirty-six percent of the total population receives some type of income support.

- Only one third of the East Harlem community have graduated from high school. Furthermore, only 10 percent are college graduates.[8]

- 23rd Police Precinct statistics covering lower East Harlem: In the seven measured crime categories, there has been a decrease in crime statistics since 1990. During 2006, there were 10 murders, 21 rapes, 322 robberies, 211 felony assaults, 91 burglaries, 274 grand larcenies and 51 grand larceny assaults.[9]

- 25th Police Precinct statistics covering upper East Harlem: In the seven measured crime categories, there has been a 67.69 percent decrease in crime statistics since 1990. During 2006 there were 9 murders, 23 rapes, 277 robberies, 237 felony assaults, 144 burglaries, 275 grand larcenies and 82 grand larceny assaults.[10]

- Those who do not consider themselves to be in good health constitute 30 percent of East Harlem residents. Heart disease is the leading cause

---

[5]Ibid.

[6]New York City Department of Mental Health, The Health of East Harlem, <http://www.nyc.gov/html/doh/pdf/data/2003nhp-manhattanc.pdf>.

[7]Community Board Eleven—Manhattan, "Statement of District Needs Fiscal Year 2007."

[8]Ibid.

[9]See "Crime Statistics: 23rd Precinct," New York City Police Department, 2007 <www.ci.nyc.ny.us/html/nypd/html/precincts/precinct_023.shtml>.

[10]See "Crime Statistics: 25th Precinct," New York City Police Department, 2007 <www.ci.nyc.ny.us/html/nypd/html/precincts/precinct_025.shtml>.

of death—45 percent higher than New York City as a whole. The district has the second highest AIDS rate in the city. The average death rate in East Harlem is 50 percent higher than both Manhattan and New York City. Approximately 12,000 years of potential life were lost before the age of seventy-five in East Harlem. East Harlem residents have a hospitalization rate that is 75 percent higher than that of all of New York City. Of the babies born in East Harlem, 10 percent are born with a low birth weight, and the infant mortality rate is higher than both Manhattan and New York City. The district's asthma rate is five times the national average. One third of East Harelm residents are overweight, and one third are obese—the highest rate of obesity in all of New York City. There are eight homeless shelters in East Harlem, three Methadone maintenance treatment programs, thirty-seven drug and alcohol treatment facilities, and thirty-seven mental health treatment facilities. These figures represent the highest concentration of shelters and facilities of any community in Manhattan and the second largest in New York City.[11]

- According to the Community Board 11 Statement of District Needs, there are primary and secondary challenges in East Harlem. The primary challenges are "the gentrification of the District, lack of affordable housing for working families, lack of commercial and retail space and the highest jobless rates in the City." The secondary challenges are having the "second highest cumulative AIDS rate" in New York City and "high levels of Asthma among the youth."[12]

MINISTERING TO YOUTH IN A STATE OF CAPTIVITY

While there have been positive developments over the past few years, the people of East Harlem continue to live under siege. Traditional youth ministry is impotent in this environment. The only way a church or parachurch organization can significantly minister to youth in this environment is through a prophetic paradigm.

While East Harlem is the profile, this community is typical of many

---

[11]Community Board Eleven—Manhattan, "Statement of District Needs Fiscal Year 2007."
[12]Ibid.

inner-city urban settings. Let us examine what this sociological and demographical study tells us about the community and how a youth ministry can respond prophetically. Try to make applications to your own unique urban context.

East Harlem is a densely populated community composed primarily of Hispanics and African Americans. Prophetic response: Instead of an all-Latino or all-African-American ministry team, develop a model leadership team which combines Latinos and African Americans. It can also offer ESL (English as a second language) classes for immigrant youth and provide Spanish-speaking resources and services for Latin American immigrants.

East Harlem has a significantly high percentage of children and teenagers. Prophetic response: Instead of focusing on youth coming to the church, bring the youth ministry to the people. Identify and intentionally plant youth ministry "outposts" in census tracts with a large population of teenagers. For example, develop a program in one of the community centers in the local housing projects.

East Harlem is composed primarily of young adults. Prophetic response: Start a young adult ministry specifically for those eighteen years old to early twenties. Keep in mind that you must be sensitive to two distinct, yet important target subgroups—college students and those who are not students. Statistically, you will have more young adults not attending college in the urban context. However, you also want to meet the needs and celebrate the accomplishments of college students. Many of these young adult college students may be the movers and shakers of tomorrow in the community.

In East Harlem, single women are the largest group of heads of households. Prophetic response: Provide resources and services for single mothers. Recognize the challenges of raising a child for a single parent. While marriage or a celibate, single lifestyle is the ideal manifestation of sexual expression in God's design, traditional churches often marginalize and judge divorced parents or people with children out of wedlock. In many urban churches, a significant number of members and people in ministry of women—and men—are divorced or single parents. In fact, based on the demographics of East Harlem, the majority of parents are single parents. Prophetic youth ministries should be compassionate and show strong support for single parents. Initiate a mentoring program or partner with an existing one. Urban youth ministries should identify and incorporate as many healthy adult role models as possible. The stories of Christian women who decided to give birth and raise their children in the face of humiliation and judgment can serve as a powerful witness for youth who are dealing with some of these very same issues.

East Harlem is a lower-income economic community suffering from unemployment. Prophetic response: Provide a food pantry. Establish a referral system for various needs. Develop support groups for unemployed parents. Offer job training and economic empowerment classes for teens and their parents.

East Harlem is a community suffering from undereducation. Prophetic response: Provide after-school programs from 3:00 p.m. to 7:00 p.m. Develop tutoring programs. Offer GED test preparation classes for those hoping to obtain a high school credential. Establish relationships with local guidance counselors. Provide SAT or ACT preparation classes for those hoping to attend college.

Crime has significantly decreased in East Harlem, but it remains an everyday reality. Prophetic response: Provide gang awareness sessions. Establish relationships with the local precinct youth officers. Offer drug awareness classes. Coordinate a trip to juvenile detention centers.

East Harlem has a heavy burden of illness and mortality. Prophetic response: Develop partnerships with health clinics. Host medical and health fairs. Provide health and nutrition education. Offer healthy sexuality training. Invite medical personnel as guest speakers. Host a sports tournament. Have an open gym night once per month.

East Harlem is being gentrified. Prophetic response: Become an advocate for families that are being forced to relocate because of rent increases. Welcome incoming families and their children to the church. Invite political leaders to address the youth and the church on community issues. Host an election candidate debate. Hold a voter registration drive.

As one can see, there are many needs in the urban context. A youth ministry can provide services for the urban community beyond those that are traditionally religious or spiritual. This is a wonderful, practical and effective way to minister to the real-life contextual needs of urban youth.

HOW SOCIOLOGY HELPS THE PROPHETIC YOUTH WORKER

- Sociology helps urban youth workers become more aware of social patterns and arrangements that shape the lives of urban youth in their communities.

- Sociology helps urban youth workers challenge conventional wisdom, popular ideas and assumptions about urban youth.

- Sociology helps urban youth workers identify social problems that affect urban youth in a particular neighborhood.

- Demographical studies and community planning help urban youth workers to strategically evaluate programming and solutions that more effectively address the needs and issues of urban youth.

BIBLICAL PERSPECTIVES ON SOCIOLOGY

The heart of sociology is *social*, understanding relationships in a larger perspective. There are many examples of social groups in the Bible. In the Old Testament, there are the Egyptians, Canaanites, Babylonians, prophets and others. The primal biblical group we encounter, however, is the Israelites. No theological understanding of Jesus is complete unless one has a social-historical understanding of the Jewish people.

> Abram fell facedown, and God said to him, "As for me, this is my covenant with you: You will be the father of many nations. No longer will you be called Abram; your name will be Abraham, for I have made you a father of many nations. I will make you very fruitful; I will make nations of you, and kings will come from you. I will establish my covenant as an everlasting covenant between me and you and your descendants after you for the generations to come, to be your God and the God of your descendants after you. The whole land of Canaan, where you are now an alien, I will give as an everlasting possession to you and your descendants after you; and I will be their God." (Genesis 17: 3-8)

In the New Testament, we are also introduced to many social groups. There are the Pharisees, Sadducees, Zealots, lepers, tax collectors, Romans and many others. But a new group, often called the people of "the Way" (see Acts 9:2; 24:14), is formed.

They devoted themselves to the apostles' teaching and to the fellowship, to the breaking of bread and to prayer. Everyone was filled with awe, and many wonders and miraculous signs were done by the apostles. All the believers were together and had everything in common. Selling their possessions and goods, they gave to anyone as he had need. Every day they continued to meet together in the temple courts. They broke bread in their homes and ate together with glad and sincere hearts, praising God and enjoying the favor of all the people. And the Lord added to their number daily those who were being saved. (Acts 2:42-47)

All the believers were one in heart and mind. No one claimed that any of his possessions was his own, but they shared everything they had. With great power the apostles continued to testify to the resurrection of the Lord Jesus, and much grace was upon them all. There were no needy persons among them. For from time to time those who owned lands or houses sold them, brought the money from the sales and put it at the apostles' feet, and it was distributed to anyone as he had need. (Acts 4:32-35)

By its very nature, relationships are social, not personal. This social-theological concept of relationships is presented from the very beginning of God's Word—relationship with God and with each other.

Then God said, "Let us make man in our image, in our likeness, and let them rule. . . ."
So God created man in his own image,
in the image of God he created him;
male and female he created them. (Genesis 1:26-27)

Many of the teachings of Jesus are social statements.

The Greatest Commandment.
"Teacher, which is the greatest commandment in the Law?"
Jesus replied: "'Love the Lord your God with all your heart and with all your soul and with all your mind.' This is the first and greatest command-ment. And the second is like it: 'Love your neighbor as yourself.' All the Law and the Prophets hang on these two commandments." (Matthew 22:36-40)

The Beatitudes.
Now when he saw the crowds, he went up on a mountainside and sat down. His disciples came to him, and he began to teach them, saying:
"Blessed are the poor in spirit,

for theirs is the kingdom of heaven.
Blessed are those who mourn,
  for they will be comforted.
Blessed are the meek,
  for they will inherit the earth.
Blessed are those who hunger and thirst for righteousness,
  for they will be filled.
Blessed are the merciful,
  for they will be shown mercy.
Blessed are the pure in heart,
  for they will see God.
Blessed are the peacemakers,
  for they will be called sons of God.
Blessed are those who are persecuted because of righteousness,
  for theirs is the kingdom of heaven.
"Blessed are you when people insult you, persecute you and falsely say all kinds of evil against you because of me. Rejoice and be glad, because great is your reward in heaven, for in the same way they persecuted the prophets who were before you." (Matthew 5:1-12)

The Golden Rule.
Do to others as you would have them do to you. (Luke 6:31)

The Lord's Prayer.
This, then, is how you should pray:
"Our Father in heaven,
hallowed be your name,
your kingdom come,
your will be done
on earth as it is in heaven.
Give us today our daily bread.
Forgive us our debts,
as we also have forgiven our debtors.
And lead us not into temptation,
but deliver us from the evil one." (Matthew 6:9-13)

Finally, always consider the milieu. For example, God speaks differently to Israel on the verge of exile from the way he speaks to Israel in exile (Jeremiah, Isaiah); Abraham's covenant promises from God were complicated in his mind by his social interactions with Pharaohs and other neighboring rulers (Genesis); Jesus' statements and the early church are set against a backdrop of a theocracy subject to military empire (the Gospels, Acts, the Epistles).

SOCIAL CAPITAL

Before we close this section, there is one last sociological principle I wish to highlight—social capital. The idea of social capital was developed by Robert Putman in his work *Bowling Alone*.[13] The central premise of social capital is that social networks have value. Social capital refers to the collective value of all "social networks" (who people know) and the inclinations that arise from these networks to do things for each other ("norms of reciprocity").[14]

Social capital highlights the benefits associated with social networks. For the middle class, these social networks are often taken for granted. A favor is called in for a family member, a connection is made for an acquaintance, or a person makes an informal recommendation for a friend's son or daughter.

Teenagers in the inner-city urban context, however, may not have much social capital. Living in the South Bronx projects, I didn't have much social capital. I didn't have adults in my life whom I could call upon to "open a door for me." Frankly, many Hispanic and black teens in the inner city don't have these social networks, much less the sophistication or abilities to negotiate these rather mature conversations.

Prophetic youth ministries serve as places where social capital is facilitated. When making a network connection on behalf of a teenager, do not be shy to introduce yourself, and say "Hello. My name is _____. I am the youth minister at _____ Church. I am calling on behalf of _____."

---

[13]Robert D. Putman, *Bowling Alone: The Collapse and Revival of American Community* (New York: Simon and Schuster, 2000). For a more comprehensive evaluation of social capital and urban youth ministry, see Bruce Main, "Zip Codes and Rolodex: Increasing the Social Capital of Urban Youth," *The Journal of Youth Ministry* 3, no. 2 (2005): 25-36.

[14]See "Social Capital Primer," Saguaro Seminar: Civic Engagement in America <www.ksg .harvard.edu/saguaro/primer.htm>.

When a teenager comes to you requesting a favor of significance, keep in mind that you may be the only person of social capital in his or her life to advocate on his or her behalf. This is the importance of having a referral list and networking. Youth ministers should make a list of contacts. A youth worker who remains isolated in an inner-city church does the youth a social-capital disservice. At the very least, youth workers should empower urban youth to speak up proactively and intelligently. They should also provide empowerment training programs and seminars.

Make an announcement from the pulpit that you wish to develop a network list for the youth ministry. Even if the church is small, you can begin to make a list. As Bruce Main explains in "Zip Codes and a Rolodex: Increasing the Social Capital of Urban Youth," if you ask even twenty people in your church to list their ten closest friends, you can generate a seed network of professional relationships. Christians who are rich in social capital can be an immense blessing to those who are poor in social capital.

Most important, youth workers should teach urban youth how to develop their own social capital. These skills should include interpersonal communications, resource research, taking notes, mentoring, leadership development and other empowering tools.

Personally, there is nothing I have accomplished in my life without the social capital support or referral of another person. I am forever grateful for these people, and I would do almost anything for them. Do you remember someone who opened a door for you?

DANGERS OF SOCIOLOGICAL EXTREMISM

Sociological extremism may supersede the dignity of the individual person. While people from the urban setting may be examined from a macro (large) perspective, each one is made in the image and likeness of God and should be treated as such. This may lead to a utilitarian-based ethical paradigm—what is best for the majority of people is what is ethically best—instead of a biblically based ethical paradigm.

Sociological extremism may lead to overgeneralizations. The irony of sociology is that while sociological analysis may present a unique picture of a particular group, it may also lead to unhelpful stereotypes and assumptions.

THE CHALLENGE OF ANTHROPOLOGY TO THE PROPHETIC YOUTH WORKER

The prophetic youth worker should become familiar with basic cultural anthropology. Prophetic theology addresses the incarnational issues of youth ministry and recognizes youth as urban. Faith in Christ saves us, and faith in Christ unites all believers. But God has incarnated each one of us in a particular racial/ethnic group, gender, language, culture and context. There is little more insulting and foolish to prophetic ears than to hear another Christian say that race does not matter. Race matters! Or, more relatedly, anthropology matters! Dismissing the importance of race is like believing that is doesn't matter that the Reverend Martin Luther King Jr. was African American. Or that Archbishop Oscar Romero was Salvadoran. Or that that Cesar Chavez was Mexican American. Or that Mahatma Gandhi was Indian. Or that Mother Theresa, Dorothy Day, Mary McLeod Bethune, Shirley Chisholm, Rosa Parks and Antonia Novello were women. Or that Jesus was Jewish. To reject, belittle or dismiss a person's anthropological identity is to reject the very incarnation of the person created in the image of God.

The nature of this topic and the limitations of this text preclude a comprehensive evaluation of race, culture and theology. Nevertheless, it must be said that it is important for the prophetic youth worker to recognize and embrace the anthropological realities of urban youth as a blessing from God.

Admittedly, certain Christian groups and congregations tend to overemphasize ethnocentrism at the expense of Christocentrism. While Christian communities need to be intentionally Christ centered, recognition of the role of race and ethnicity is a matter of basic demographics. Frankly, there simply are not too many white sisters and brothers living in or visiting the inner city, except in areas where gentrification is on the rise. And, yes, inner-city churches must intentionally reach out to our white and Asian sisters and brothers living in the urban context. However, to deny the gifts, struggles, realities and uniqueness of one's cultural heritage is an insult to the community and to the Creator who incarnated us. This is especially the case when certain minority groups have historically and systematically been told that their anthropological incarnation is inferior, even sinful.

HOW ANTHROPOLOGY HELPS THE PROPHETIC YOUTH MINISTER

Let's be honest. Inner-city urban youth ministry in North America is primarily Christian ministry to poor Hispanic and black teens. On the one hand, it is unfair to expect the field of youth ministry, which is primarily white, middle-class and suburban, to fully comprehend the anthropological realities of the inner city without living among us. On the other hand, it is dismissive of the field of youth ministry to continue to present a melting-pot, global youth culture philosophy and pastoral theology which seems irrelevant to the realities of the North American inner-city youth ministry.

Prophetic youth ministry does not dis-incarnate the Gospel message from the anthropological realities of urban youth. This would be dichotomizing the human person—removing the Spirit from the body. Anthropology informs theology. How can it not? The power of the gospel is the Word incarnated among a specific people in a specific place in a specific time throughout the world. If the Word is not incarnated to the realities of a people, then it is irrelevant. The good news is not a philosophical or generic treatise; rather, it is the life, death and resurrection of Jesus being relived, retold and reborn again and again among the people. The gospel is transcultural and incarnational, but it is not a melting-pot gospel. The gospel is global *not* because it is generic but because it is incarnated, birthed within the dignity of each and every group of people.

I once coordinated a youth outreach in the South Bronx. A few weeks prior to the event, I attended a Pentecostal church and heard a young man playing the electric guitar singing a beautiful contemporary Christian hymn. I introduced myself and was pleased to find out that he had a band. He shared his incredible testimony with me of how Christ saved him from witchcraft and Satanism. I invited him to be our guest speaker at this outdoor event attended primarily by Hispanic and black teens. Naïvely, I also invited his band to perform without listening to a demo of their music. The event was going well until the band started to play. While they were an excellent Christian band, their music was pure hard rock. The teens who expected hip-hop, gospel or Latin music, made the best of the event. But I learned, very quickly, the importance of the relationship between theology and anthropology. Knowing your target audience is not just a ministry strategy; it indicates that you understand and respect the unique cultural preferences of the group. In this case, the music selection reflected an insensitivity to and lack of appreciation for the target audience. Although this was certainly not my intention, the music actually became an obstacle to hearing the gospel message.

Hip-hop is the language of inner-city youth. It is raw and unadulterated poetry which speaks of the pain and struggles of urban living. Admittedly, many of the lyrics of hip-hop music are offensive and demeaning; however, they need deconstruction, require wise exegesis and should be placed in their social-cultural context. The prophetic youth worker speaks the language of the urban youth. Of course, you should not interpret this literally. I am not suggesting that youth workers should act or speak like teenagers. There is little more foolish than adults acting like teenagers. Effective urban youth workers, however, embrace and integrate the gospel message with the language of urban culture. Calenthia Dowdy eloquently explains,

> Rap music has served as a tool for telling these sorts of stories. Stories of the lives of oppressed people rarely seen or acknowledged. They are the invisible underprivileged, hidden away in pockets of despair while others are privileged by not having to see them or feel their pain. These are the stories of modern day poor folk, orphans, widows and aliens in their communities.
>
> Current youth ministry must release and empower its young prophets, encouraging them to speak and act regarding both moral and social righteousness. They are young prophets in your midst. It would not be wise to discourage them from learning about and speaking about structural evil that systematically represses certain segments of society.[15]

Liberation theology, Latino theology, black theology, Asian theology, feminist theology and womanist theology all speak about God from their unique anthropological and incarnational perspectives and suffering. These voices represent perspectives often marginalized within the body of Christ. While they absolutely reflect a sociological dimension, they also share anthropological commonalities—racial and gender marginalization. While a prophetic youth worker should remain faithful to biblical and

---

[15]Calenthia S. Dowdy, "Voices from the Fringes: A Case for Prophetic Youth Ministry," *Journal of Youth Ministry* 3, no. 2 (2005): 94-95.

Christian orthodoxy, he or she must also recognize and advocate on behalf of marginalized groups.

It is also essential to recognize intracultural differences. I must admit that I have never fully understood the animosity between certain Latino groups in the city. Yet, this expresses the distinct needs of each group. Puerto Ricans, Dominicans, Mexicans, Columbians, Salvadorans and others are different from one another. Urban youth ministers must be cautious to avoid the foolhardy tendency to overgeneralize a certain group of people, for example, because they share a common language.

I have also seen this principle in the black community. African Americans, West Indians, Africans, European blacks, black Hispanics and others each have different needs and issues even though they share common racial features. This is also applicable in the Asian community. It is simplistic and insulting to assume that Koreans are the same as Chinese, Japanese and others from East Asia.

Finally, there are also generational considerations. First-generation youth arriving in the United States will have certain needs distinct from second-generation youth who were born and raised in the United States. Each group reflects a certain dignity and incarnational reality. The prophetic youth worker must be aware of and sensitive to these cultural and generational factors. First-generation youth will need services and ministry to help them adjust to the realities of the United States. For second-generation youth, these issues may not be applicable or are simply taken for granted.

As one can see, a basic appreciation of anthropology offers the prophetic youth worker a better and deeper understanding of inner-city youth. Anthropology helps the youth worker to become more familiar with and sensitive to God's people and their distinct culture in a particular context.

BIBLICAL PERSPECTIVE ON ANTHROPOLOGY

Traditionally, the story of the Tower of Babel is told from a negative perspective. It is viewed as God's condemnation of the greed and self-aggrandizement of a people who share a common language building a monument to themselves. God's negative solution: God confuses their language and scatters them throughout the world.

But notice how the story changes when told from a more anthropologically positive perspective. God recognizes the sinful pride of this monocultural and monolingual people. God's positive solution: God initiates cultural and linguistic diversity throughout the world. Anthropological diversity is the solution, not the curse, to the sin of self-centered cultural pride. This serves as both a warning and exhortation to all races and ethnicities that God shows no partiality.

> Now the whole world had one language and a common speech. As men moved eastward, they found a plain in Shinar and settled there.
>
> They said to each other, "Come, let's make bricks and bake them thoroughly." They used brick instead of stone, and tar for mortar. Then they said, "Come, let us build ourselves a city, with a tower that reaches to the heavens, so that we may make a name for ourselves and not be scattered over the face of the whole earth."
>
> But the LORD came down to see the city and the tower that the men were building. The LORD said, "If as one people speaking the same language they have begun to do this, then nothing they plan to do will be impossible for them. Come, let us go down and confuse their language so they will not understand each other."
>
> So the LORD scattered them from there over all the earth, and they stopped building the city. (Genesis 11:1-8)

In *Where the Nations Meet,* Stephen Rhodes quotes Walter Brueggemann, who explains the distinction between divine unity and human-made unity.

> There are two types of unity. On the one hand, God wills a unity which permits and encourages scattering. The unity willed by God is that all of humankind shall be in covenant with him and with him only, responding to his purposes, relying on his life-giving power. Then there is the unity suggested by this passage: "a different kind of unity sought by fearful humanity organized against the purposes of God. This unity attempts to establish a cultural, human oneness without reference to the threats, promises and mandates of God. This is a self-made unity in which humanity has a "fortress mentality." It seeks to survive by its own resources. The focus of humanity is on self-interest, not on obedience to God.[16]

---

[16]Stephen A Rhodes, *Where the Nations Meet: The Church in a Multicultural World* (Downers Grove, Ill.: InterVarsity Press, 1988), pp. 25-26.

Rhodes reminds us that in Genesis 10, the writer records the descendents of Noah through his three sons. In the lineage of Japheth, we read, "From these the maritime peoples spread out into their territories by their clans within their nations, each with its own language" (Genesis 10:5). Diversity existed prior to the story at Babel. Therefore,

> God's judgment on Babel is the fulfillment of what humanity hoped to prevent: its scattering. . . . The judgment is twofold: (1) the diversity of languages is restored as God had originally intended; and (2) humanity is again spread across the earth so that the people may "multiply and fill the earth." God's judgment in Babel may not be seen solely as punishment, for in the divine act of scattering humanity, God's original intention for humanity and creation is fulfilled.[17]

If one fast-forwards to Pentecost, we see the thread in which the power of the Holy Spirit is given to the church through unity in a common spiritual language (speaking in tongues), yet expressed through a multicultural and multilingual reality. As Ray Bakke writes, "For the first time, under the influence of the Holy Spirit, all those languages were used in worship in Jerusalem. From then on the Church's worship would be multilingual in the heart of the city where one language was official but many others were spoken by the people."[18]

> When the day of Pentecost came, they were all together in one place. Suddenly a sound like the blowing of a violent wind came from heaven and filled the whole house where they were sitting. They saw what seemed to be tongues of fire that separated and came to rest on each of them. All of them were filled with the Holy Spirit and began to speak in other tongues as the Spirit enabled them.
>
> Now there were staying in Jerusalem God-fearing Jews from every nation under heaven. When they heard this sound, a crowd came together in bewilderment, because each one heard them speaking in his own language. Utterly amazed, they asked: "Are not all these men who are speaking Galileans? Then how is it that each of us hears them in his own native language? Parthians, Medes and Elamites; residents of Mesopotamia, Judea and Cappadocia, Pontus and Asia, Phrygia and Pamphylia, Egypt and the parts of

---

[17]Ibid., pp. 24-27.
[18]Ray Bakke, *A Theology as Big as the City* (Downers Grove, Ill.: InterVarsity Press, 1997), p. 139.

Libya near Cyrene; visitors from Rome (both Jews and converts to Judaism); Cretans and Arabs—we hear them declaring the wonders of God in our own tongues!" Amazed and perplexed, they asked one another, "What does this mean?"

Some, however, made fun of them and said, "They have had too much wine." (Acts 2:1-13)

While speaking in tongues is certainly a spiritual gift, the greater point here is unity through spiritual oneness, not through a cultural or linguistic homogeneity. In *Christian Existence Today*, Stanley Hauerwas comments,

> It is only against the background of Babel . . . that we can understand the extraordinary events of Pentecost. . . . The tribes, learning their languages, were now reunited in common understanding. . . . At Pentecost God created a new language, but it was a language that is more than words. It is instead a community whose memory of its Savior creates the miracle of being a people whose very differences contribute to their unity. We call this new creation, church.[19]

Anthropologically different youth ministries reflect the cultural diversity of the body of Christ. Although certain urban youth ministry models seem to be raised above others, all are equally valid. The apostle Peter was initially hesitant to recognize the dignity of the Gentiles. The hypocrisy of Peter's logic was the fact that although he was a great sinner, he still promoted a traditionalistic, exclusivistic, parochial and legalistic manner of treating people who did not fit into his monocultural model. It wasn't until his convicting vision and after living in the home of Cornelius, a God-fearing Gentile, that Peter changed his perspective. Peter had to live with the Gentiles in order to understand and love Gentiles. He states, "I now realize how true it is that God does not show favoritism but accepts men from every nation who fear him and do what is right" (Acts 10:34-35).

It seems to me that part of the reason why most North American youth ministry models do not connect with urban youth workers is because they were neither consummated by urban people nor birthed in the urban con-

---

[19]Stanley Hauerwas, *Christian Existence Today: Essays of Church, World, and Living in Between* (Durham, N.C.: Labyrinth, 1988), p. 53.

text. Certainly, God uses certain people to go to other lands to minister. Abraham, for example, left Ur and eventually settled in Canaan (Genesis 12:1-7). Many believers who are not urban residents feel called to minister in the city. It is the Moses story, however, which seems to reverberate most among urban churches. A native son, wanted by the ruling authorities for murder, rejects the political structure, returns to his roots and leads a revolution among his people. Obviously, the overwhelming majority of urban youth workers come from the urban context. While this is primarily a sociological demographic reality, there are also anthropological theological considerations. That is, effective urban models must be consummated by urban youth leaders and birthed in the urban context.

In the Hebrew Scriptures, God instructs the Israelites to select a leader who is anthropologically and theologically like them. Perhaps God is instructing urban Christians today to do the same. "Be sure to appoint over you the king the LORD your God chooses. He must be from among your brothers. Do not place a foreigner over you, one who is not a brother Israelite" (Deuteronomy 17:15).

While I am *not* suggesting an ethnocentric youth ministry leadership model, I *am* suggesting a Christocentric model which is incarnationally appropriate and anthropologically sensitive. Unfortunately, most youth ministry models are neither. They seem to be cookie-cutter models which are culturally and anthropologically neutral.

Nevertheless, ultimately it is our faith in Christ, not our race, culture or ethnicity, which gathers us as a people of God and grants us salvation. Heaven, it seems to me, will be multicultural and multilingual, but one in the Spirit.

> For we were all baptized by one Spirit into one body—whether Jews or Greeks, slave or free—and we were all given the one Spirit to drink. (1 Corinthians 12:13)

> There is neither Jew nor Greek, slave nor free, male nor female, for you are all one in Christ Jesus. (Galatians 3:28)

> Here there is no Greek or Jew, circumcised or uncircumcised, barbarian, Scythian, slave or free, but Christ is all, and is in all. (Colossians 3:11)

DANGERS OF ANTHROPOLOGICAL EXTREMISM

- Anthropological extremism may lead to an ethnocentric youth ministry orientation instead of a Christocentric youth ministry orientation.

- Anthropological extremism may lead to a perpetualization of presumptions and stereotypes of certain groups. This may lead to continued prejudices and discrimination.

- Anthropological extremism may have a reverse effect by creating animosity and antagonism between different groups instead of a better understanding and more fruitful dialogue with one another.

- Anthropological extremism may develop a narrow, specific and culturally limited theological perspective at the expense of a broader, universal and transcultural one.

10

Defining *Radical*

RADICAL EDUCATION AS PROPHETIC MINISTRY

The word *radical* offers several different meanings which are helpful in better understanding radical education. First, young people use *radical* as a slang term to mean excellent or cool: "That's radical, dude!"[1] Second, *radical* is defined as a considerable departure from the usual or traditional: "That theory is too radical." *Radical* also has political implications; in the United States, people who are viewed as extremists on either side of the American political spectrum are often identified as *radical*—the radical left (liberal perspective) or the radical right (conservative perspective). This is also seen in church politics. Certain churches or denominations are viewed as radically conservative or radically liberal.

The etymology of the word *radical* has to do with the "fundamental root." To be truly radical is to reconnect to the roots of something that's become overgrown and departed from its own origins. A prophetic youth ministry should be radical in that it should radically educate its youth, undergirding them in the fundamentals of Christian truth and how they connect to life. The prophetic youth worker should become familiar with basic radical education. Prophetic theology addresses the political issues of youth ministry and recognizes young people as prophets. Prophetic youth ministry weaves four educational curriculum ideologies: religious

---

[1]"Radical" in *Merriam-Webster Online*, <www.m-w.com/cgi-bin/dictionary?book=Dictionary&va=radical&x=13&y=15>; accessed June 15, 2005.

orthodoxy, cognitive pluralism, progressivism and critical theory.

THE CHALLENGE OF RADICAL EDUCATION TO THE PROPHETIC YOUTH WORKER

The first ideology is *religious orthodoxy*. This combines religion with education. There are at least five features of religious orthodoxy. The first one is the belief in the existence of God. Second, religious orthodoxy tends to have a sacred text, a written word with God's message for humanity. For Christians, this is the Holy Bible. Third, it has a specific interpretation or theology that explains God's message and a specific spirituality that demonstrates how one should live out this interpretive theology. While Christians are united in Christ, there are various interpretive perspectives, such as evangelical, Pentecostal, Roman Catholic, reformed, Anglican/Episcopal, Lutheran, Eastern Orthodox and others. Fourth, it believes that the theological/spiritual curriculum cannot be separate from the academic curriculum.[2] In other words, what we believe and what we learn cannot be divorced from how we live. Finally, the academic curriculum of religious orthodoxy—aims, content, method and evaluation—is informed by its theological/spiritual interpretations.

Because the prophetic youth ministry is transdenominational, each tradition or denomination develops and informs its own orthodox perspective.

Cognitive pluralism promotes the educational concept that there is a plurality of knowledge and intelligences.[3] While this theory has been developed more intentionally and popularly in Howard Gardner's *Frames of Mind: The Theory of Multiple Intelligences*[4] and Daniel Goleman's *Emotional Intelligence*,[5] this concept has roots that extend back to Aristotle, who identified three different forms of knowledge—theoretical, practical and productive.[6]

Cognitive pluralism transforms *intelligence* from a noun into a verb.

---

[2]While all of life serves as a curriculum for learning and education, the separation of spiritual curriculum from academic curriculum is simply presented as a descriptive to highlight the integration of theology/spirituality and education.

[3]For a more detailed examination of these curriculum ideologies, see Elliot W. Eisner, *The Educational Imagination: On Design and Evaluation of School Programs,* 3rd ed. (Upper Saddle River, N.J.: Merrill Prentice Hall, 2002), esp. pp. 47-86.

[4]Howard Gardner, *Frames of Mind: The Theory of Multiple Intelligences* (New York: Basic Books, 1983).

[5]Daniel Goleman, *Emotional Intelligence: Why It Can Matter More Than IQ* (New York: Bantam, 1995).

[6]Eisner, *Educational Imagination,* p. 79.

That is, according to Eisner, "intelligence is not merely something you have, but something you do."[7] Gardner identifies seven intelligences, which each person possesses to varying degrees. They are linguistic, musical, logical-mathematical, spatial, body-kinesthetic, intrapersonal and interpersonal.

Eisner explains, "For Gardner, these are not 'simply' aptitudes or talents, but socially important ways of solving problems. Furthermore, he argues that environmental conditions have something to do with the particular kind of intelligence that will be valued and practiced."[8]

Previously, we examined the staggering rates of poverty, immigration and limited education in East Harlem. Considering these realities, how does cognitive pluralism inform youth ministry in the urban context? First, it challenges the youth worker to teach in nontraditional ways. For the urban youth worker, it is possible that many of the youth present in Sunday school or the religious education program may not be literate. Therefore, how can we teach the truth of the Bible and the Christian faith to an undereducated, illiterate student audience? While this may seem defeating at first, cognitive pluralism suggests and encourages ways of teaching beyond the traditional perspectives.

Second, cognitive pluralism suggests that students are intelligent beyond the traditional ways of knowing. Therefore, Sunday school, youth ministries and religious education programs which measure Christian intelligence using traditional school-like tests and

Questions to Ponder

Do youth in the urban context think intelligently and process knowledge in different ways from their middle-class or suburban youth counterparts? And, if so, is not the traditional IQ way of measuring intelligence an inconsistent or faulty tool to properly evaluate other ways of knowing? Finally, if youth are intelligent and think differently from their middle-class or suburban counterparts, should there be different ways of measuring spiritual intelligence and discipleship? Is there only one way to become a disciple of Christ?

---

[7]Ibid., p. 81.
[8]Ibid.

memorization techniques may actually be marginalizing many students who are intelligent in other ways. More significantly, it may perpetuate the shame and frustration a teenager feels in school and insinuate these feelings into their faith. This could lead a young person to the terrible thought that, "Not only am I stupid in school, but I'm also stupid in church." I would certainly suggest eliminating any test-type of measurements and challenge urban youth workers to "think outside the box" and teach in more nontraditional ways that are appropriate for these young people.

Finally, it is also vital for the urban youth worker to recognize that there are essential differences between Eurocentric learning styles and the learning styles of people of color. This is particularly significant since the overwhelming volume of youth ministry resources come from a white and middle-class pedagogical perspective. In *Cognitive Styles and Multicultural Populations*, James Anderson offers some helpful distinctions.[9] See table 10.1.

Table 10.1. Cultural Learning Style Differences

Eurocentric	*People of color*
Distant	Closer/relational
Fact centered (depersonalized)	Story centered (social)
Critical thinking	Rote learning (needs application)
Internal standards	Needs praise and support
Field independent	Field dependent
Dichotomous	Holistic
Extracts key ideas	Does not extract key ideas
Theory oriented	Imagery oriented
Time centered	"Elastic" time
Conjunctive concepts	Disjunctive concepts

[9]James Anderson, "Cognitive Styles and Multicultural Populations," *Journal of Teacher Education* 39 (1988): 2-9. See also Donald Ratcliff, "Psychological Foundations on Multicultural Religious Education," in *Multicultural Religious Education*, ed. Barbara Wilkerson (Birmingham: Religious Education Press, 1997), pp. 93-128.

Questions to Ponder

Do the unique stressors of urban life—particularly within inner-city urban communities—unduly affect the academic learning and personal/spiritual development of urban youth? Do the socioeconomic obstacles experienced by many urban youth interfere with their learning abilities? Are teachers familiar with and do they utilize the various learning styles and intelligences which may be more effective for the academic well-being of urban youth?

While one may disagree with various points on Anderson's list, it nevertheless highlights the realities of what many urban youth workers have been saying for decades: urban youth think and learn differently, and, therefore, the available youth ministry resources are generally disconnected or irrelevant to urban youth ministries.

Furthermore, adding to this discussion on cognitive pluralism, beyond the intellectual perspective is the emotional quotient (EQ). Goleman convincingly argues that having an emotionally healthy outlook is a more effective determining factor for life's success than the traditional intelligence quotient (IQ).[10] The emotional well-being of a person will undoubtedly influence the person's intellectual well-being. We begin to see the interrelatedness between the personal and the academic dimensions of this curriculum.

"There is no thinking without feeling and no feeling without thinking. The more conscious one is of what one is experiencing, the more learning is possible. Experiencing one's self in a conscious manner—that is, gaining self-knowledge—is an integral part of learning."[11]

Furthermore, the emotional health of the learning environment has a significant impact on the intellectual learning of the student. John Steinberg correctly writes, "The 'emotionally safe' classroom is logically a classroom where more learning can take place. The 'social environment' of a school highly determines the ability of the students to concentrate on school work."[12]

---

[10]See Goleman, *Emotional Intelligence.*

[11]Karen Stone-McCown, Joshua M. Freedman and Marsha C. Rideout, *Self-Science: The Emotional Intelligence Curriculum,* 2nd ed. (San Mateo, Calif.: Six Seconds, 1998), p. ix.

[12]John Steinberg, "The History of Affective Education," *EQ Today,* Winter 1998 <http://www.eqtoday.com/archive/jpca.html>.

Integrating the ideology of cognitive pluralism into urban youth ministry accomplishes at least three objectives. First, it recognizes the diversity of learning and welcomes student-disciples of various intelligences. Second, it incorporates techniques and tools that are sensitive to various learning styles and intelligences, such as small-group projects, arts and crafts, or music. Third, it helps to shatter the negative perceptions, often imposed on and conditioned by urban youth, by explaining not only that people learn differently (inferred from an understanding of learning styles) but that they are intelligent in ways other than the traditionally measured IQ. Naturally, this liberating concept has revolutionized the educational system and pedagogical theory and encourages youth who may have been labeled underachievers or special needs students.

Progressivism. Progressivism is rooted in two educational concepts. The first is the nature of human experience and intelligence. The second is social reform.[13] Many contemporary progressive educators view these two streams as reflecting the personal and the political.[14] John Dewey, the father of progressive thought, believed the classroom should reflect democratic principles.[15] The classroom should allow students the space, opportunity and freedom to formulate their individual beliefs. Personal needs and uniqueness must be respected, and group processes should be encouraged to foster dialogue, nurturing students toward positive social engagement.[16]

Questions to Ponder

As Christian educators, urban youth workers should ask themselves, Do I create an environment which is emotionally healthy?

Do youth in Sunday school or youth ministry feel safe asking questions, or do they feel shamed? Is the teaching environment emotionally healthy or dogmatic and legalistic? Are students allowed to question freely, or are they silenced or shamed? Are the teens in the youth ministry growing emotionally healthy or emotionally unhealthy?

---

[13]Eisner, *Educational Imagination*, p. 67.
[14]Ibid.
[15]See John Dewey, *Democracy and Education* (New York: Macmillan, 1916).
[16]Eisner, *Educational Imagination*, pp. 67-73.

The first challenge to the prophetic youth worker is, Does your classroom reflect a democratic or autocratic environment? Unfortunately, I have observed, too often, sessions where the teacher did not approve of alternate perspectives, group discussions or questioning of the content material. The prophetic youth worker embraces these moments as opportunities for deeper reflection and more passionate faith-building exercises.

In *Pedagogy of the Oppressed*, Paulo Freire identifies the banking concept of education.[17] The banking concept dangerously promotes the idea that knowledge is a gift bestowed by those who consider themselves knowledgeable upon those whom they consider to know nothing. Unfortunately, this is often the case in an undemocratic classroom environment. This projection by the teacher is characteristic of the ideology of oppression; it negates true educational learning. Freire describes the teacher utilizing the banking concept as follows:

- The teacher teaches and the students are taught.

- The teacher knows everything and the students know nothing.

- The teacher thinks, and the students are thought about.

- The teacher talks and the students listen—meekly.

- The teacher disciplines and the students are disciplined.

- The teacher chooses and enforces his choice, and the students comply.

- The teacher acts, and the students have the illusion of acting through the action of the teacher.

- The teacher chooses the program content, and the students (who were not consulted) adapt to it.

- The teacher confuses the authority of knowledge with his or her own professional authority, which he or she sets in opposition to the freedom of the students.

- The teacher is the subject of the learning process, while the pupils are mere objects.[18]

---

[17]Paulo Freire, *Pedagogy of the Oppressed,* 30th anniversary ed. (New York: Continuum, 1993), pp. 71-86.

[18]Ibid., p. 73.

While Paulo Freire's philosophy of education reflects mainly the radical educational ideology of critical theory, Freire also promotes a pedagogical method consistent with progressivism—the teacher-learner relationship, dialogue praxis and problem-posing education.[19] The teacher stands in solidarity and in equality with the students. He or she is a sojourner learning as well, and in conversation with the students. The teacher, therefore, is also a student, learning with and not lording over the students. Furthermore, the teacher can suggest themes, but not determine or control the dialogue.

Progressivism emphasizes the problem-centered concept.[20] That is, the teacher constructs an educational environment where students formulate problems or problematic situations. The students are then encouraged and provided the conditions to formulate resolutions to the problems. The prophetic youth worker in the urban context does not have to formulate problems in the classroom. Following Freire's thought, together the prophetic youth worker and students begin with the investigation of the cultural situation. In this case, the cultural situation is the urban context filled with problems which youth experience everyday. The cultural situation provides the curriculum of problems that are discussed. These experiences are examined in light of God's Word and God's world and lead to social action.

The primary metaphor for progressivism is growth. The growth and development of the student includes both the resources of the academy and the resources of culture.[21] What good is an education if the students cannot interact with the culture and do not make a positive contribution to society? What good is a youth ministry if it does not develop Christians who can do these things?

Prophetic youth ministry incorporates four major principles from the progressive ideological tradition. First, it empowers youth and young adults to grow—personally, academically, spiritually and socially—transforming both themselves and their communities. Second, it presents transformation as a lifelong and ongoing process of greater becoming. Third, it invites youth and young adults to identify and explore problematic situa-

---

[19]John L. Elias and Sharan B. Merriam, *Philosophical Foundations of Adult Education,* 2nd ed. (Melbourne, Fla.: Krieger, 1995), p. 156.
[20]Ibid., p. 70.
[21]Eisner, *Educational Imagination,* p. 68.

tions—personally, academically, spiritually and socially—and encourages them to formulate resolutions to these problems. Finally, it challenges youth and young adults to become more engaged in community and civic involvement.

Questions to Ponder

How do the youth in your youth ministry respond to problem situations? Do inner-city urban youth respond differently to problems from the way middle-class or suburban youth respond? Does your youth ministry employ a banking method or a more progressive or liberational method of teaching? Is your teaching style democratic or autocratic? Are the young adults who leave your youth ministry contributing to society?

Critical theory. Critical theory is a curricular ideology which engages in the hermeneutical exegesis of the values, assumptions and hidden agenda which underlie education in particular and society in general.[22]

Eisner tells us that "Critical Theory pulls back the veil of social and cultural life. It uncovers and unmasks the data, the figures, and 'texts' that shape life. It questions issues of power and decodes power relationships. Critical Theory seeks a truer democracy. It critiques the silencing of speech and desires a more authentic dialogue."[23]

In *The Educational Imagination*, Eisner examines three curricula that every school, classroom and teacher teach—the explicit curriculum, the implicit curriculum and the null curriculum.[24] The explicit curriculum, in the classroom or in society, is the explicit or clearly expressed course of study written on the syllabus of the course, or on the syllabus of life, such as newspapers, television or radio. This is the information that is known and promoted.

The implicit curriculum is the curriculum that is taught indirectly. This is informed by and reflects the patterns and authorities in the dialogue. Perhaps certain people, in the classroom or in society, are allowed to speak much while others speak little. Why is this? The texts that are selected for

---

[22]Ibid., pp. 73-77.
[23]Insight offered by Dr. Kieran Scott in the class Curriculum Development and Religious Education, Fordham University Graduate School of Religion and Religious Education, April 29, 2004.
[24]Eisner, *Educational Imagination*, pp. 87-107.

the classroom or for society are intentionally political; that is, they reflect the subjective bias of the teacher or the people in power. What is implied by the selection of these texts? Schools teach far more than they advertise.[25] John Dewey also argues that we learn more than what we are directly taught.[26]

But not all implicit curriculum is bad. For example, schools and youth ministries implicitly teach many positive social values not in an explicit curriculum—punctuality, hard work, delayed gratification, respect.

Critical theory would surely explore the implicit curriculum of the classroom and of society. But it is most concerned about the null curriculum or hidden curriculum. This reflects the censored subject material, the books left out of a course, the social texts censored from the cultural conversations. This, too, is political because it reflects the subjective bias of the teacher or the people in power. Censorship is not neutral. What is not taught is as important as, perhaps even more important than, what is taught. The hidden curriculum implies something that was intentionally concealed.

One of the most important questions from a critical theoretical perspective is, "Whose interests are being served?"[27] In the classroom, it is the teacher who both selects and censors the material. In society, it is the people in power. In the conversation of injustice, it is the oppressor.

Paulo Freire asks this central critical question toward transformation, "How can the oppressed . . . participate in developing the pedagogy of their liberation?"[28] Any issue which oppresses, marginalizes or silences is an object for critical reflection.

Freire argues that the oppression of any person dehumanizes both the oppressor and the oppressed. The oppressors are unable to liberate themselves or the oppressed, because this would mean the loss of power and possessions from the "possessing class." For the oppressors,

> having more is an inalienable right, a right they acquired through their own
> "effort," with their "courage to take risks." If others do not have more, it is

---

[25]Ibid., p. 92.
[26]Dewey, *Democracy and Education*, pp. 18-19.
[27]Eisner, *Educational Imagination*, p. 74.
[28]Freire, *Pedagogy of the Oppressed*, p. 48.

because they are incompetent and lazy, and worst of all is their unjustifiable ingratitude towards the "generous gestures" of the dominant class.[29]

Even the self-discovery of the oppressor as an oppressor, Freire continues,

> may cause considerable anguish, but it does not necessarily lead one to solidarity with the oppressed. Rationalizing his guilt through paternalistic treatment of the oppressed, all the while holding them fast in a position of dependence.[30]

> Only power that springs from the weakness of the oppressed will be sufficiently strong to free both. Any attempt to "soften" the power of the oppressor in deference to the weakness of the oppressed almost always manifests itself in the form of false generosity; indeed, the attempt never goes beyond this.[31]

Perhaps Freire's greatest contribution to our understanding of radical education in relation to prophetic youth ministry is the concept of *conscientization*. Conscientization, which reflects both an intellectual understanding and personal awareness within a social context, is true knowledge. It is true knowledge of reality because it is connected with reflective (thinking) activity and praxis (action). Individual liberation and societal liberation are closely tied together in this theory.[32] The gospel message flowing from youth ministries should therefore be a message which speaks of a total liberation—spiritual, personal and social. As Mary John Manazan explains, salvation should be viewed "as the liberation of the whole human being . . . liberation not only from sin, death and hell, but from everything that dehumanizes him (and her) including oppression, exploitation, injustice and dehumanizing poverty."[33] Prophetic youth ministry leads to conscientization.

Youth living in the urban context have developed a keen critical hermeneutical suspicion of the implicit and hidden curricula that surround them. They ask the same questions as the critical theorists: Whose interests are

---

[29]Ibid., p. 59.
[30]Ibid., p. 49.
[31]Ibid., p. 44.
[32]Elias and Merriam, *Philosophical Foundations*, p. 151.
[33]See Manazan's statement quoted in Gregory F. Augustine Pierce, *Activism That Makes Sense: Congregations and Community Organization* (Skokie, Ill.: ACTA, 1984), p. 8.

being served? Whose voices are being silenced? Who is invited into the conversation? Who is left out and why? Who are the people in power? Who are the powerless?

Prophetic urban youth ministries deconstruct and can read between the lines. In addition to the developmental changes of adolescents and the challenges of youth culture, they have to negotiate between the spiritual needs of youth and the social realities of the urban context. Critical theory invites youth to discuss issues in the implicit and hidden curricula of their lives and their communities. It also teaches them, in keeping with the Christian faith and biblical principles, how to critically reflect and act on these issues, engaging in social transformation.

HOW RADICAL EDUCATION HELPS THE PROPHETIC YOUTH WORKER

- Radical education helps the urban youth worker to think more critically.
- Radical education helps the urban youth worker to confront assumptions.
- Radical education challenges the urban youth worker to move beyond memorization and simplistic responses.
- Radical education challenges urban youth workers to move beyond the "chalk and talk" educative teaching style to a more democratic teaching-learning style where every youth member has a voice.
- Radical education challenges urban youth workers to be not only teachers but students as well.
- Radical education teaches the urban youth worker how to hermeneutically exegete culture, community and church.
- Radical education helps the urban youth workers to identify hidden agendas.
- Radical education helps the urban youth workers to identify the voiceless, who is being silenced and what issues are being avoided.
- Radical education equips and empowers urban youth workers to help voiceless youth develop their own voice.
- Radical education helps biblically orthodox urban youth workers to integrate evangelism and social action.

- Radical education challenges youth workers to construct and proclaim a gospel message of total liberation—spiritual, personal and social.

BIBLICAL PERSPECTIVES ON RADICAL EDUCATION

There are many Scripture passages which deal with knowledge and the importance of learning. But perhaps the single most poignant passage reflecting the spirit of radical education comes from the very voice of God, who expresses the anguish which so many urban ministers feel as they minister in situations of captivity: "My people are destroyed from lack of knowledge" (Hosea 4:6).

This heartfelt expression serves as a challenge and rallying cry for urban youth workers to become more engaged in the transformation of urban communities through the radical education of our youth. Our young urban people indeed are being destroyed from lack of knowledge. It is only through the radical education of a prophetic youth ministry that we can foster a spirit of knowledge, discernment and action.

Prophetic youth workers understand that the kingdom of God is not just a spiritual construct. For its contextual realization, it also comes through power. "For the kingdom of God is not a matter of talk but of power" (1 Corinthians 4:20).

"Power tends to corrupt; absolute power corrupts absolutely." These words from Lord Acton have long expressed the danger of autocratic power. There is no doubt that radical education confronts people, systems and structures that hold power. The oppressor represents the power of one over another. For many Christians, the idea of confronting powers and principalities remains an otherworldly, spiritual battle. However, to keep this understanding of power in the realm of the heavens is a misunderstanding of the struggles against powers and principalities on earth. It is a perpetuation of the faulty division between the sacred and the secular.

The bottom line is that the poor and marginalized reflect the powerless of our society. Radical education is an education—a conscientization—toward giving the powerless more power. Prophetic youth workers have the right, indeed the duty, to proclaim justice and to denounce injustice in the name of Jesus Christ, our great liberator. Unfortunately, many youth ministries and churches are uncomfortable reflecting critically about injustice, much less taking action against it. Richard Johnson writes,

> We must examine, therefore, our aversion to the use of power. . . . [I]t is the realization that power means responsibility. If I have power, I am obligated to use it on the behalf of good. I deny the existence of my power lest I be called on to employ it. Thus the flight from power is really the flight from responsibility.[34]

Power in and of itself is amoral. It is simply the capacity to act. Listen once again to the prophetic words proclaimed from the Urban Family Empowerment Center, a faith-based organization located in the Bronx whose mission is "to holistically empower urban families." These thoughts reflect the interaction of the power of Christian faith and radical education in the urban context.

> We believe people are created in the image and likeness of God and recognize the sacred dignity of human life at every stage. While people are capable of great good, we are marred by an attitude of personal disobedience toward God called sin.
>
> Furthermore, beyond personal sin there also exist social, economic, and political sins that create systemic injustice which oppresses people and demeans human dignity.
>
> Any injustice or disrespect for human life is an affront to God. Therefore, all of creation is in need of liberation, reconciliation, and redemption that can only be found through the life, death, and resurrection of Jesus Christ.
>
> While all people are in need of God's love and healing, we are uniquely concerned about the urban family, particularly the poor, and stand in solidarity with them. Therefore, we humbly yet boldly accept the call to be a lighthouse, spiritually and socially, in the urban community, sharing the Good News of Jesus Christ, engaged in personal, spiritual, and social transformation, and committed to the struggle of justice.[35]

Another example that expresses the spirit of righteous anger and ac-

---

[34]See Pierce, *Activism That Makes Sense*, p. 33; Richard Johnson, *Reflections of Self-Interest and Power: A Theological Justification for Community Organization* (Saint Paul: Twin Cities Organization, n.d.), p. 3.

[35]The Urban Family Empowerment Center, founded by this writer, was conceived in response to the increasing needs of lower-income, inner-city families. Birthed in the South Bronx, it is a private, not-for-profit, faith-based organization whose mission is to holistically empower urban families <www.empowerthefamily.org>.

tion that flows out of radical education is the story of Jesus clearing the temple.

> When it was almost time for the Jewish Passover, Jesus went up to Jerusalem. In the temple courts he found men selling cattle, sheep and doves, and others sitting at tables exchanging money. So he made a whip out of cords, and drove all from the temple area, both sheep and cattle; he scattered the coins of the money changers and overturned their tables. To those who sold doves he said, "Get these out of here! How dare you turn my Father's house into a market!" (John 2:13-16)

Jesus' action here is directed both to the religious and to the political authorities. Not only does this express a theological statement—Jesus is *the* Lamb of God who takes away our sins—it is also a radical action against the religious and economic structures which often take advantage of people, particularly the poor.

People were required to make sacrifices for their sins. Many who made the long journey could not bring their animals. Some who brought their animals were rejected because their animals had imperfections. The price of a sacrificial animal in the temple area was usually much higher than elsewhere. Money changers and merchants had to pay taxes, so they would often charge exorbitant rates.[36] Frequently, the poor were unable to purchase the better-quality animals, leaving them with disappointment and shame.

Prophetic youth workers see the injustice and confront the systems, even at the expense of being considered radical. Dom Helder Camara, Roman Catholic Archbishop of Recife, Brazil, famously said, "When I feed the poor, they call me a saint. When I ask why the poor have no food, they call me a communist."

Jesus' clearing of the temple occurred twice. The first time is stated above. The second time is written in Matthew 21:12-17, Mark 11:12-19 and Luke 19:45-48. This story models the political expression necessary for youth ministry and the prophetic role of youth.

---

[36]See footnotes for John 2:13-16 in *Life Application Study Bible: New International Version* (Carol Stream, Ill.: Tyndale; Grand Rapids: Zondervan, 1991), p. 1875.

DANGERS OF RADICAL EDUCATION EXTREMISM

- Radical education extremism can lead to an overdeconstruction of the Truth. The revelation of God, in Jesus Christ through the power of the Holy Spirit, as expressed through the Holy Bible is an absolute truth which cannot be deconstructed into a simple myth or negotiable theoretical construct.

- Radical education extremism can lead to an unhealthy cynicism. It can also lead to the frustration and danger of perpetual questioning in which nothing seems assured, even salvation.

- To traditionalists, prophetic youth workers will seem too radical and too revolutionary.

- To liberals, prophetic youth workers will seem too conservative for believing in the absolute truth of God's revelation in Jesus Christ through the power of the Holy Spirit.

- To social activists, prophetic youth workers will not seem radical enough for their commitment to a biblically orthodox social justice over against a secular humanistic utilitarian social justice.

PART THREE

Urban Youth Workers

11

The Subway

One brisk autumn morning, I waited for the subway train to arrive at the elevated 238th Street train station of the Bronx. The tracks were being repaired. Like most New Yorkers waiting for the train to arrive and seeking to occupy their time, I watched transfixed as a group of courageous people worked on the subway tracks. Suddenly, I envisioned an urban image for prophetic youth workers.

The subway train represents teens engaged in youth culture. Youth culture is a powerful moving locomotion which comes at full speed, from both directions. And, as trains often do, it arrives at varying times, so you have to be flexible. When the train arrives, you can walk in or watch it go by. Sadly, many urban youth ministries watch the train go by. Prophetic youth workers get on the train.

The men and women working on the tracks represent Christians who work with youth. They are laying a strong foundation. Others are conductors who drive the train, while maintenance workers clean the subway system. A prophetic youth ministry needs a strong team of mature and healthy adults who can lay a strong foundation for youth, lead the way and help sanitize the often murky environment of youth culture.

The other passengers on the train represent people, as well as conglomerates, entities, organizations and systems which fill the youth culture train. Unfortunately, many of them have agendas or values which are not consistent with Christian biblical values. Therefore, while many of our Christian bystanders watch the train go by, other passengers board the train, promoting their values and developing relationships with our youth. We need more healthy adult Christians on the train.

The third rail gives the power of the Holy Spirit. Traditionally, the third rail represents the most dangerous aspect of the subway system. It is commonly known that stepping on the third rail surely means death by electrocution. Yet, the third rail also represents power. Without this power, the subway system would shut down. For the prophetic youth ministry, the third rail reflects the power of God. And, it reminds us that urban youth ministry is situated on holy ground which requires us to stand respectfully and fearfully.

Finally, I noticed the watchperson. The watchperson had a whistle to notify the workers of any danger and to inform the conductor to proceed with caution. In one hand, the watchperson carried a megaphone and spoke to the workers, guiding them, informing them, encouraging them and, when necessary, correcting them. In the other hand, the watchperson held a walkie-talkie radio speaking with, presumably, superiors and colleagues giving updated information. Most significantly, the watchperson continuously looked backward and forward, over and over again.

The prophetic youth worker is like the watchperson, vigilant of the incoming youth culture train. He or she guides, informs, encourages and corrects the workers, making sure that a strong foundation is being laid and that the teens are being led appropriately. He or she is up to date on the latest information regarding youth trends. Most importantly, the prophetic youth worker is continuously looking backward to the traditions and history of the Christian faith, yet looking forward to the future.

THE PROPHETIC YOUTH WORKER AS SPIRITUAL AND SOCIAL PROPHET

In "Theological Framework for Youth Ministry: Repentance," Robin Maas writes, "The prophet is always herald, witness and guide. His word, his works and his person all bear witness to a reality that is beyond him, to something, someone else."[1] The author then connects John the Baptist

---

[1]This section is greatly informed by Robin Maas, "Theological Framework for Youth Ministry: Repentance," in *Starting Right: Thinking Theologically About Youth Ministry,* ed. Kenda Creasy Dean, Chap Clark and Dave Rahn (Grand Rapids: Zondervan, 2001), pp. 229-41.

Table 11.1. Watching the Trains: An Urban Image for Prophetic Youth Workers

Train Images	*Youth Ministry*
Train	Youth culture
Track workers	Youth ministry workers
Passengers	Youth and other competing interests
Third rail	Power of the Holy Spirit
Watchperson	Prophetic youth worker

with Elijah, a prophet of messianic significance, and Malachi, a prophet of social justice significance.

John the Baptist serves as the archetype for prophetic youth workers who are committed to holistic urban youth ministry, integrating evangelism and social action. Prophetic youth workers deal with the struggles of sharing a spiritually and contextually relevant gospel with urban youth, all the while sifting through the myriad issues of poverty, broken families, violence and other urban challenges. For the prophetic youth worker, the language of spiritual warfare is not solely related to spiritual matters, but also relates to their battles with the social ills that bind many young people, such as drug use, promiscuity and risky behavior.

THE PROPHETIC YOUTH WORKER POINTS YOUTH TO CHRIST

While John the Baptist challenged people to change their ways, at no point did he ever take any credit or desire any fame. He recognized his limited role and unworthiness, while always pointing to Christ: "After me will come one more powerful than I, the thongs of whose sandals I am not worthy to stoop down and untie. I baptize you with water, but he will baptize you with the Holy Spirit" (Mark 1:7-8).

Like the prophets, the youth workers too must be herald, witness and guide—always pointing to Christ. They must point to Christ not only for theological reasons, but also to relieve themselves from the self-induced professional stress and messianic delusion of being the savior of youth. This is significant for urban youth workers, who are overwhelmingly bi-vocational—ministering in the church while working and raising a family. They are under stress, expected to succeed in ministry with little financial and programmatic support.

THE PROPHETIC YOUTH WORKER, A SPIRITUAL PROPHET

In those days John the Baptist came, preaching in the Desert of Judea and saying, "Repent, for the kingdom of heaven is near." This is he who was spoken of through the prophet Isaiah:

"A voice of one calling in the desert,
'Prepare the way for the Lord,
make straight paths for him.'" (Matthew 3:1-3)

John the Baptist was certainly not shy about challenging people to look at their own hearts and change their ways. While we may not necessarily be as confrontational as he was, urban youth workers must not compromise the gospel message either. On the one hand, traditional youth workers might want to avoid being overly dogmatic and legalistic in matters of evangelism. On the other hand, liberal and activist youth workers must neither fear nor neglect their primary responsibility of sharing the gospel message and pointing youth to Jesus Christ.

Youth respect transparency, authenticity, relevancy and love. At the death of Pope John Paul II, thousands upon thousands of young people around the world celebrated the life of this traditionally orthodox Catholic leader. Youth's respect for authenticity was also apparent in the 2005 Billy Graham crusade in New York City. Thousands of the participants were young persons who energetically worshiped Jesus Christ, as well as celebrated the life of this evangelical leader.

Regardless of the popular postmodern notion that young people do not believe in moral absolutes, it is clear that young people *do* respect transparency and authenticity. Young people respected Pope John Paul II and Billy Graham for their integrity even if they did not necessarily agree with everything these two men taught. Youth also appreciated the love these two religious leaders seemed to have for young people.

Youth will listen to and respect an urban youth worker who boldly shares the gospel message if the youth worker is also transparent, authentic, relevant and loving. I am often asked, "Why do you think there are so few youth in urban churches?" Rhetorically, I usually respond, "Is your church/youth ministry transparent, authentic, relevant and loving when it comes to urban youth?"

As I mentioned in the early part of this book, the city is filled with ineffective youth ministries run by wonderful and dedicated Christians. Often, these saintly people simply do not come across to youth as adults who can be trusted with the secrets and struggles of adolescence, are relevant to contemporary youth culture, or are particularly friendly. My hope, of course, is that after reading this book, urban youth workers will have a better grasp of how to develop into more effective prophetic youth workers.

I believe that one of the reasons contemporary evangelical and conservative Christian churches/youth ministries are growing while liberal mainline churches/youth ministries are not is because of their commitment to, or at least attempt at, being transparent, authentic, relevant and loving to youth, while unapologetically standing for Christ and a biblically orthodox perspective.

The adolescent worldview is in a constant state of flux and identity formation. A prophetic youth worker, like John Paul II and Billy Graham, can serve as a lighthouse in the stormy years of adolescence.

THE PROPHETIC YOUTH WORKER, A SOCIAL PROPHET

> But when he saw many of the Pharisees and Sadducees coming to where he was baptizing, he said to them: "You brood of vipers! Who warned you to flee from the coming wrath? Produce fruit in keeping with repentance. And do not think you can say to yourselves, 'We have Abraham as our father.' I tell you that out of these stones God can raise up children for Abraham. The ax is already at the root of the trees, and every tree that does not produce good fruit will be cut down and thrown into the fire." (Matthew 3:7-10)

Unquestionably, John the Baptist was a spiritual prophet who challenged people to repent and change their ways. But he was also a social prophet, publicly confronting the hypocrisy of religious leaders (Pharisees and Sadducees) and political leaders (Herod), even referring to them as a "brood of vipers." These challenges to the religious and political power systems ultimately led to his death.

The urban youth worker too must be a social prophet. As examined in the previous chapters, urban youth workers must critically exegete the structures and systems which oppress or neglect urban youth. Urban youth seem naturally attracted to social prophets. Unfortunately, not all social prophets are spiritual prophets in the biblical sense. Just as traditional youth workers tend to be natural spiritual prophets (emphasizing evangelism), activist youth workers tend to be natural social prophets (emphasizing social action). A prophetic youth worker is holistic, integrating both evangelism and social action.

A PROPHET YOUTH WORKER RECEIVES NO HONOR

> When Jesus had finished these parables, he moved on from there. Coming to his hometown, he began teaching the people in their synagogue, and they were amazed. "Where did this man get this wisdom and these miraculous powers?" they asked. "Isn't this the carpenter's son? Isn't his mother's name Mary, and aren't his brothers James, Joseph, Simon and Judas? Aren't all his sisters with us? Where then did this man get all these things?" And they took offense at him.
>
> But Jesus said to them, "Only in his hometown and in his own house is a prophet without honor."
>
> And he did not do many miracles there because of their lack of faith. (Matthew 13:53-58)

A prophetic youth worker must accept the lifelong cross that he or she is a prophet who receives no honor. From the right, traditionalists will not feel comfortable with the prophetic youth worker's seemingly over-involvement in social justice activities and challenges to religious, political and cultural traditions. From the left, liberals and activists will not feel comfortable with the prophetic youth worker's seemingly zealous enthusiasm with Jesus Christ, the Bible and moral absolutes. Prophetic youth workers will undoubtedly feel that they are not understood in their hometowns or houses. Although prophetic youth workers never become accustomed to this constant state of battle, they accept this burden in fidelity to the prophetic way.

A popular maxim states, "If you want to be a bridge between people, prepare to be stepped on from both sides." There is much truth to this reality for prophetic youth workers. Of course, they are not trying to appease everyone, but trying to faithfully live up to the prophetic life in Jesus Christ.

Ultimately, joy and affirmation for the prophetic youth worker come

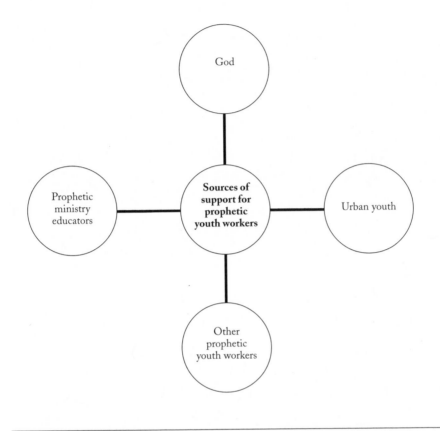

Figure 11.1. Sources of support for prophetic youth workers

from four sources. The first two are God and urban youth. From God comes the blessing, "Well done, good and faithful servant!" (Matthew 25:21). From urban youth comes the appreciation of incarnation ministry—living and struggling with them.

The second two sources are other prophetic youth workers and prophetic ministry educators. I cannot overemphasize the importance of prophetic youth workers reaching out and seeking fellowship with each other. Based on my experience and conversations with other prophetic youth workers from the urban context, they never feel 100 percent comfortable in a gathering of traditional, liberal or activist youth workers. This is particularly true in denominational and national youth leadership gatherings that are overwhelmingly representative of middle-class or suburban youth ministries. Prophetic youth workers have expressed a disconnect, non-acceptance or dismissiveness of their urban perspectives from many of their middle-class and suburban counterparts.

Prophetic ministry educators, especially youth ministry educators, are also a source of support. Often, these educators are currently involved in ministry or have many years of ministry experience, as well as formal academic training. As previously mentioned, the blessing of academicians is their gift to analyze, criticize and theorize about the prophetic dimension. Their contributions help youth workers to re-envision youth ministry. These educators may be in the fields of youth ministry, pastoral ministry, Bible, theology or Christian education. However, educators at Christian colleges or ministry institutes may also be supportive of prophetic youth ministry. It is vital for the life and energy of the prophetic youth worker to draw strength from these four sources of support, particularly because he or she often feels alone in ministry.

A FINAL WORD

The purpose of this book was to offer a theoretical and methodological framework for youth ministry in the urban context. My prayer is threefold: (1) that prophetic youth workers in the urban context feel affirmed, empowered and energized to continue this most holy and important work; (2) that traditional, liberal and activist youth workers consider moving toward becoming more prophetic youth workers; and (3) that urban youth ministries in cities around the world transform into dynamic and holistic prophetic youth ministries addressing the spiritual, personal and social needs of urban youth. Amen.